Lynn Jurewicz AND **Todd Cutler**

high tech
high touch

Library
Customer
Service
through
Technology

American Library Association
Chicago
2003

While extensive effort has gone into ensuring the reliability of information appearing in this book, the publisher makes no warranty, express or implied, on the accuracy or reliability of the information, and does not assume and hereby disclaims any liability to any person for any loss or damage caused by errors or omissions in this publication.

Composition by ALA Editions in Sabon and Optima using QuarkXPress 5.0 on a PC platform

Printed on 50-pound white offset, a pH-neutral stock, and bound in 10-point cover stock by Victor Graphics

The paper used in this publication meets the minimum requirements of American National Standard for Information Sciences—Permanence of Paper for Printed Library Materials, ANSI Z39.48-1992. ∞

Library of Congress Cataloging-in-Publication Data

Jurewicz, Lynn.
    High tech, high touch : library customer service through technology /
by Lynn Jurewicz and Todd Cutler.
      p. cm.
    ISBN 0-8389-0860-8
    1. Libraries and the Internet. 2. Public services (Libraries)—Technological innovations. 3. Customer services—Technological innovations. 4. Library Web sites. I. Cutler, Todd. II. Title.
    Z674.75.I58J87 2003
    025.5′24—dc21   2003010087

Printed in the United States of America

07   06   05   04   03   5   4   3   2   1

Contents

Figures

Preface

Today's librarian cannot think about libraries and technology without thinking of the wise, if somewhat curmudgeonly, words of Walt Crawford. "Technology does not define libraries. . . . Technology is a tool. . . . Libraries should serve their communities."[1] He has written these words so often they are now almost synonymous with his name. This book provides a perspective on the library service ethic through the use of specific technologies.

As author partners, we bring the complementary experiences of directing a public library along with computer programming and systems design. We set out to resolve marketing and communication issues at the Mooresville Public Library in 2000 with the grant-funded design of the automatic e-mail notification system for new items and programs described in chapter 3. This project grew out of disappointment with pre-designed library automation vendors' "solutions" which did not fit the problems that staff and patrons were facing. We saw that the concepts of the e-mail notification system could be used to design solutions for other common library problems, and several of the other systems described in this book evolved from it. We have spoken at library conferences about the success of our efforts, and have been inspired by the enthusiasm in the field for projects of this sort. We describe systems that evolved from the experiences of librarians needing to adapt to various library issues and policies.

Libraries across the United States are now beginning to meet service objectives through the use of digital libraries, portals, e-mail notifications, and database interfaces to the Web. Many of these systems were created in-house, to solve specific library problems. Some of these solutions are becoming available as turnkey systems from large library vendors, but typically they are not uniquely tailored to individual libraries.

This begs the question of who should drive the technology in libraries. Do libraries expect vendors to design all of the solutions? Are libraries limited to an array of solutions designed for business? The narrative descriptions and screen shots in this book are intended to serve as a springboard for the design of customized library systems that address unique local service issues. Step-by-step directions with computer code are beyond the scope of this book, but the ideas provided here allow library personnel at all levels to consider how technology can be used as a tool to improve customer service. The systems described in this book may inspire some of the people "on the fence" to consider custom-designed solutions. The concepts detailed here may give tech-savvy library system administrators an insight into how similar web pages could function for their own systems, or they may give them ideas for other systems. They may inspire children's services managers and their staffs to take a shot at designing a system to capture the program statistics they need while streamlining their registration processes. At the least, the concepts in this book may give others, such as circulation managers and library marketing staff, ideas about what is out there and provide them with the incentive to seek out those with the technological skills to make it happen.

It can be difficult to take a blank canvas and turn it into a painting without some type of image in mind. While some may be content to simply purchase a painting off the shelf, others will want to create a masterpiece that matches their own personal style. This book strives to create a vision of customer service for staff and patrons that can be achieved through the use of technology. We hope the models that we present might inspire your masterpieces.

Note

1. Walt Crawford, "Finding Stability in Changing Times," *Online* 24, no. 2 (March/ April 2000): 52.

1 Libraries on the Internet

Rationale and Issues

As the last decade of the twentieth century came to a close, most libraries had established a presence on the World Wide Web. The content provided on these websites included details of the library's physical plant and staff and, in the best of cases, the online catalog. Today, however, it is not enough to merely provide a link to the library catalog. Library websites are quickly becoming a key piece of the information delivery system. As the scope of data widens, the significance of the library catalog has slipped sharply in terms of the variety of information that customers demand; this is due simply to the limited scope of information that the catalog can deliver. There are limitations to search engine capability because so much of the information is stored in catalog databases inaccessible to search engines.

Widely accessible technologies like cell phones and MP3 and DVD formats have created a new breed of library patron who demands services that are outside traditional catalog searching. This patron counts among his expectations such multimedia technologies as personal communications, entertainment, and even personal record-keeping. Libraries must consider expanding the technical resources available from their sites to fulfill the information expectations of these savvy patrons in their communities. It is no longer enough to assume that an Internet presence alone proves a library's commitment to accessibility. Patrons are looking for convenience as well as excellent service, and they are looking for convenience across the board in their daily routines. If we truly want to be part of our patrons' daily routines, libraries must provide convenience along with our more common claims to relevancy and accessibility.

As librarians, most of us would argue that the library was never just a place to store books and provide access to them. Libraries have diversified from their traditional services to offer multiple formats, highly creative programs, online reference service and homework help, meeting room reservation and rental, computer labs, electronic newsletters, and homegrown electronic databases. Library administrators are managing larger facilities, larger staffs, and broader arrays of programming and services. Circulation and program staffs are juggling additional record-keeping tasks and attempting to track patron activity across the broadening service spectrum. Access to localized information resources such as those supporting local history and genealogy is becoming increasingly unwieldy, as local collections have reached critical mass in the last decade. All library procedures in place to deal with these services have been affected by technology, whether libraries have already transitioned their services or are in some phase of transition.

INFORMATION SHIFTING

This is the same transition that Jenny Levine of "The Shifted Librarian" website calls "information shifting": "I took the name from a presentation that I do called '*Information Shifting*' about how the change from pursuing information to receiving information is and will be affecting libraries."[1] Levine reflects on what she perceives to be the key difference between the Baby Boomers and the Internet Generation, which is that the NetGens expect information to come to them. The value of selectively focused information streams increases as we are bombarded with information from all directions. The Internet has given us a variety of tools that provide for the distribution of information over a large area both inside and outside the library. These tools include not only web pages but e-mail, online newsletters, indexes, and search engines. The tools that the Shifted Librarian advocates are those that help to make the library more "portable," that allow us to reach customers in new or better ways. As our communities become more sophisticated technologically, they look to us to provide them with technical avenues into the library. We have seen in our own lives that as customer habits have changed, savvy businesses have changed their service strategies in an attempt to anticipate customer needs. . . . Too busy to go to the mall? Buy from a catalog online and we'll send it to your door. Need to know when to update your online auction bid? Sign up for our service and we'll notify you. Want to know where your package is? Check our website and we'll track it for you. Consumers can electronically (and instantly) exchange information without having to search for their shoes or car keys, or even dial the phone. Good business is about accessibility and convenience and great service. In some cases that means faster service; in some cases it means convenient or even automatic service. Great service can usually be defined as delivering what was promised; excellent service involves delivering more than what was expected, and must involve the anticipation of customer needs as well. Technology tools through the Internet provide libraries with the avenues to offer such personal and convenient, even "automatic" library service.

INTERNET USE ON THE RISE

It seems superfluous to say that the last three or four years have seen a huge growth in Internet use. In the last six months of 2000, the number of adults with Internet access increased by 16 million.[2] By the end of that year, 58 million Americans were logging on to the Internet each day, an increase of 9 million from just six months earlier. A 2002 Pew study cites 60 percent of Americans as now having Internet access and 40 percent of Americans as having been online for more than three years.[3] The online community has grown dramatically, and users are increasingly comfortable with search strategies, electronic forms, and other applications. Consumer routines include online purchasing, electronic surveys and discount coupons, and purchase circles. For example, purchase circles on Amazon.com provide the titles of uniquely popular items to specific groups of customers. Amazon identifies the groups by zip code and domain name, and looks at their collective purchases against the purchases of the general population. Customers can check the purchase circles of their hometown, their alma mater, or their local government.

"Push technology" has expanded consumer expectations through applications like AvantGo automatic updates and eBay bid alerts. AvantGo software provides automatic website updates directly to your PDA (personal digital assistant), while eBay's bid alert service will send you an automatic message that you have just been outbid on that irresistible item you simply must have. Growing numbers of consumers are comfortable with checking their bank balances online. E-mail newsletters and electronic discussion lists are common across many fields as a way to keep up with important topics. In short, online services have become ubiquitous for Internet users. The proliferation and growing ease of use of these services in business have created an expectation among the general public for similar services from nonprofit service providers. The expectation is that nonprofits will not only have a web presence but will contribute new and valuable services for the nonprofit sector. Staying relevant to modern consumers is a survival strategy for both businesses and nonprofit organizations. As service providers, libraries will need to maintain a service continuum similar to that of profitable businesses.

The idea that everyone goes to the Web first for information these days is a persistent concern among librarians. Jones *e*-global library surveyed public, school, and academic libraries in December 2001 to determine how librarians characterize their work in this digital environment, as well as how they predict their work will change in the future.[4] The survey return group was fairly evenly comprised of school, public, and academic librarians. Survey respondents are spending on average about 50 percent of their research time on the Internet at present. That amount increased to 60 percent when respondents were asked to predict how much research time they will spend dealing with Internet resources in the next two years, with school librarians predicting they would spend 70–75 percent of their time thus. When asked what the most significant challenges are for librarians in the future, all three groups agreed that the perception that "everything's on the Web" is the principal challenge facing librarians. That concern was shared by 80 percent of public librarians, 90 percent of school librarians, and 92 percent of academic librarians.

As access to the Internet has begun to fade as an issue, customers view web-based research as the information resource path that is strewn with the fewest obstacles. The Internet is the research tool of choice for students everywhere now. Despite misinformation, redundancy, poor organization, and overwhelming numbers of hits, the numbers show that users prefer to turn to the Web first for research.

Aggressive efforts to assimilate technology and the Internet into schools nationwide have contributed to this phenomenon. In 2001, 94 percent of online teens used the Internet for school research and 71 percent used the Internet as the major source for their most recent school project.[5] As our customers have transitioned their information-seeking behaviors to the Web, libraries everywhere have seen increasing traffic on their websites.[6] The perception that the Internet can provide everything that the patron needs, along with the need to survive what is widely perceived as the "Amazon crunch," have driven many libraries to reconsider their service strategies and positioning. Information delivery in the form of online reference services, profile-based automatic e-mail systems, and customized portals to digital resources are just a few of the methods libraries are employing to organize the information glut.

> This [convenience] catastrophe is nothing more or less than the disappearance of our print collections in the face of more easily obtained digital content. . . . Once our clients begin to see the Internet as the answer to all or most of their questions, our sources of support will be in jeopardy. —Roy Tennant[7]

PERSONALIZATION OF ONLINE SERVICES

The concept of personalization is likely to drive expansion in new library web services and products.[8] Consumers are demanding relevancy and timeliness, but librarians do not aspire to be telemarketers for the information we provide access to; we don't want to press unwanted information on unwilling consumers in a random way. Personalized gateways like MyYahoo and individually selected PDA downloads from AvantGo illustrate consumers' demand for limiting data delivery to that with personal relevancy. Netflix, the web-based DVD subscription service, has a "recommender" function that suggests other titles to members based on the ratings of movies they have already viewed. Likewise, Amazon's pervasive self-marketing techniques are built on making personalized suggestions for purchases that are based on customer profiles. As libraries have recovered from their initial fears over Amazon's explosive appearance in the reading marketplace, anxiety over the Amazon crunch has changed to respect for the "Amazon effect."[9] Amazon led the way to Internet success by offering ease of use, quick delivery, a personal recommending service, and multiple ways to access items in its gigantic database.

Libraries worried in the 1990s that the Amazon catalog model pointed out the shortcomings of many online public library catalogs, and that the Amazon business model would likely have ramifications for the service expectations of library customers. As circulation plunged in the face of computers and Internet access, anxiety about the future of traditional library services rose. Fifty-one percent of the respondents in *Library Journal*'s "Book Report 2000" survey reported a decrease in adult circulation, and 95 percent of the respondents blamed the Internet.[10] In the face of the Internet and online booksellers, libraries worried about the virtual library leaving them in the dust.

On the other hand, libraries have benefited from the Amazon model in that they are working hard to develop and market new services to better meet customer demand. New consumer expectations have created new roles for librarians and new products and tools in the information chain. If librarians start thinking in terms of using the new tools and start considering how people are actually using them (as opposed to how techies and vendors want them to use them), they can develop customized applications that will extend their mission. Customized technology applications in libraries can be used to support libraries' larger mission in much the same way that businesses use technologies to support their bottom line.

Technology can be compared to library furniture. We look for furniture that is multifunctional. It must be a good investment and enhance the invitation to our customers to feel welcome. Its appearance makes a statement about the library's purpose and services. We believe libraries need to inspire new kinds of technology "furniture." Instead of just choosing from a catalog, or copying the furniture we already have, we should let the vendors know what our design criteria are and purchase or design the best models to fit our needs.

Notes

1. "The Shifted Librarian" (home page of Jenny Levine), available at http://www.theshiftedlibrarian.com/stories/2002/01/19/whatIsAShiftedLibrarian.html (accessed 3 January 2003).
2. Pew Internet & American Life Project, "Getting Serious Online," 3 March 2002, available at http://www.pewinternet.org/reports/toc.asp?Report=55 (accessed 12 December 2002).
3. Pew Internet & American Life Project, "Counting on the Internet," 29 December 2002, available at http://www.pewinternet.org/reports/toc.asp?Report=80 (accessed 9 January 2003).

4. Jones *e*-global library, "The Role of Librarians in the Digital Age," 2001, available at http://www.jonesknowledge.com/eglobal/pdf/ala_survey_results.pdf (accessed 14 November 2002).

5. Pew Internet & American Life Project, "The Internet and Education," 2001, available at http://www.pewinternet.org/reports/toc.asp?Report=39 (accessed 9 January 2003).

6. Barbara Hoffert, "Book Report 2000: Circulation Dips but Buying Still Up," *Library Journal* 125, no. 3 (15 February 2000): 130.

7. Roy Tennant, "Digital Libraries—The Convenience Catastrophe," *Library Journal* 126, no. 20 (15 December 2001): 39–40.

8. Tom Kochtanek, "New Developments in Integrated Library Systems," *Library Technology* (November 2001), available at http://gessler.emeraldinsight.com/vl=9528114/cl=114/nw=1/rpsv/librarylink/technology/nov01.htm#article (accessed 29 November 2002).

9. Barbara Hoffert, "Book Report 2002: The Amazon Effect," *Library Journal* 127, no. 3 (15 February 2002): 38.

10. Hoffert, "Book Report 2000," 130.

2 What Libraries Can Learn from Business

Survey data shows that people feel that they need to be on the Web. In a recent issue of *American Libraries,* U.S. Secretary of State Colin Powell was quoted as remarking to the President's Council of Advisers on Science and Technology, "I no longer have any encyclopedias, any dictionaries, or any reference materials anywhere in my office, whatsoever, I don't need them. I've stopped using all reference materials because you don't need it. All you need is a search engine."[1] If the Internet will indeed be able to fulfill the promise of replacing printed reference materials, libraries will need to catch up with what businesses are doing in order to capture a "market share" of the web activity our customers are choosing to participate in.

In the wake of the Internet explosion, customers expect their suppliers to use the Internet to keep them informed. Customer demand drives the growth of such services as personalized e-mail messages. The expectation is that corporate websites will provide up-to-the-minute information to consumers. It's important to note that customer expectations are dynamic, and expectations change over time. Businesses know that they need to continually update their service and marketing strategies, and updated company information is critical. Additionally, as businesses add services to their websites they add marketing value by providing ever more reasons for customers to visit them there.

As service-driven companies have utilized technology to improve customer service, they have also used technology to improve internal processes. Libraries are frequently challenged to provide more services while keeping costs low, as are many businesses. We are accustomed to focus on customer services, occasionally at the risk of adding more staff and often at the risk of adding more work for existing staff. While many businesses likewise value a customer focus, they also systematically evaluate internal processes to see where they can be more efficient and do more with less.

Libraries are no less committed to streamlined operations, but tradition and funding issues have made for a long ride on the change curve for many of them. As libraries become more comfortable with the corporate concepts of process mastering and system engineering, it becomes easier to identify those areas within our service domain that are potential areas for change. Technology services and products are natural alternatives for increasing the speed and accessibility of many library procedures.

THE BUSINESS MODEL

The term "business model" describes the combination of processes that make up a corporate identity. It refers to the positioning of a product or service in the value chain. Examples of business models vary widely and dramatically. In the simplest models, a business produces a product and sells it. If the business does a good job of producing, marketing, and delivering the product to a receptive target audience, these costs are lower than the selling price and the company realizes a profit. Businesses typically strive to run lean in order to increase profit margins, and they routinely engage in self-evaluation to achieve that goal. If customer service is a critical component of a corporation's business model, the business also engages in service evaluation and tries to find a balance between running lean and keeping customers happy. This business model is similar in some ways to the service ethic of libraries.

The explosion of the Internet has significantly changed many business models. The Internet medium has provided for the development of new models that were not previously possible. The easy access and convenience of Internet services are terrific marketing tools to attract customers, but they can also improve internal processes. Shipping giant FedEx now woos customers through such web services as offering a 10-percent savings on all express shipping orders placed online. FedEx also provides online order tracking, e-mail shipping and delivery notifications, and an online address book that stores up to 1,000 addresses. The FedEx Invoice Online service is an Internet bill presentation and bill payment application. With this service, payments can be scheduled via electronic funds transfer, and reports can be downloaded from the website. Customers can also schedule a FedEx pickup online. All of these options simplify key procedures for FedEx's customer base. Shifting the provision of basic critical services to the Internet streamlines FedEx's internal procedures by simplifying routine service tasks.

The Marshall Field Company did away with "task-interfering duties" for sales personnel. This retailer implemented automated check approval and in-house telephone directories to speed communication between departmental units and other stores. The modifications resulted in streamlined checkout and better customer service. The task-based processes that were modified had been time-consuming and prevented staff from responding to customer requests.[2] Tasks can be standardized by replacing the task components with technology, improving the methods by which the tasks are completed, or a combination of the two. Technology is at its most successful in simplifying services when it is used to handle routine or standardized transactions. When customer service staff are relieved of routine or repetitive transactions, they can concentrate their efforts on personal interactions with customers.

In another example, computer manufacturer Gateway's business model has changed from the provision of telephone support to the provision of two new technical support options. The first is technical support e-mail submission, which offers the option of an automatic extraction of system information as a forms page loads and the customer gives permission for the extraction. The newer tech support option is Gateway's 24/7 Chat with Tech Support, which provides live chat with tech support personnel. The "chat assistant" pushes the information that best answers your question to the left side of your screen, while he chats with you on the right side of the screen. A complete transcript of the session, as well as any links that were pushed to you by the chat assistant, is e-mailed to you at the conclusion of the session to eliminate the need to print out the information during the chat session. Gateway Customer Service will also engage in chat with customers seven days a week on customer service issues. Providing online technology services to a technology customer base may seem like a no-brainer. But the evolution of customer service from a phone-based service to a web-based service utilizing real-time chat is a good example of how the Internet has changed a corporate business model.

Other examples of Internet technologies that have changed business models include software downloads, patches, updates, software trials, and online product registrations. The utilization of push technology for the provision of automatic virus-protection software updates is a common practice that has dramatically simplified an industry process. In "push" technology, users choose the types and levels of data to be automatically "pushed" to their individual computers, PDAs, or other devices. Push technology was a hot topic in 1997 and was conceived as a constant unselected download, but it suffered from its requirement of huge bandwidth and other issues. The concept of push technology has resurfaced in new formats, however, and while it has influenced corporate business models for some time, public libraries are just beginning to see its value for library application development. Both the electronic discussion lists that we love and the pop-ups that we love to hate are examples of push technology. In the case of automatic virus-protection updates, the update is automatically pushed to the consumer's computer on a regular basis, eliminating the need for customer log-in and request. Both the customer and the company benefit from a process that has been restructured by shifting it to an Internet service.

Text messaging is an Internet technology with a growing impact on business models that use data communications technologies to interact with customers. Text messaging is an Internet Protocol-based method for communication between people using various devices. The most popular text messaging medium today is between computers and is commonly known as "instant messaging," but the technology is also used to send short messages of usually a hundred characters or less between wireless phones. Internet instant messaging is an ideal medium for customer service. Heavily used by both teens and many businesses, instant messaging provides real-time communications and opportunities for collaboration without long-distance telephone charges. By 2005 it is expected to be integrated into 50 percent of the applications used by businesses to communicate with customers.[3]

Text messaging has had an impact on library service as well. The real-time chat component of online reference service is transforming the reference model. Online reference services where customers can connect with a staff member via the Internet to get reference help are becoming increasingly popular. Growing numbers of libraries are adopting a 24/7 online reference-desk service in order to step up the level of reference access to customers. Online reference is provided through customizable software tools that enable the librarian to direct the patron's browser, send files to his computer, and conduct meetings with multiple participants. Services can be accessed through the Web, and require that customers have a direct Internet connection and the ability to use Java applets.

The Starbucks coffee chain recently equipped 1,200 of its locations with wireless Internet access, with 70 percent of its locations worldwide expected to provide access to customers by 2005.[4] Through a partnership with Hewlett-Packard and T-Mobile, Starbucks customers can be more comfortable than ever in the big chairs with their coffee. Some libraries are offering a similar service, by providing wireless network access to staff and running DHCP (Dynamic Host C Protocol) networks. Customers are asking libraries to allow them to access the Internet and other network applications with their own laptops equipped with wireless cards. DHCP randomly and automatically assigns an Internet Protocol (IP) number to devices logging onto the network. This provides access to the network, as opposed to static IP addresses, which require that each device on the network "own" an IP number as part of its network setup information. Although this new technology introduces new security vulnerabilities, the wireless service possibilities are intriguing.

While wireless Internet access may not dramatically change the way that Starbucks does business, it provides one more reason for its customers to be there and to purchase Starbucks's products. Services like wireless Internet access at Starbucks will contribute to the increasing array of online options that drive customer expectations for services in other venues.

The same consumers who are using the Internet to save time and access business data are also patrons of public libraries. Many forward-looking libraries are taking a cue from the corporate world by borrowing from the corporate model of technology-based process mastering. Process mastering is a key tool to record each piece of a process as it occurs, including inputs, outputs, and each step of the process. The purpose is to provide a method to standardize a procedure in order for it to be evaluated and improved. Benefits include "cost reduction, increased productivity, improved safety, higher morale and the ability to meet the changing expectations of your customers."[5] As library professionals, we are looking at key processes especially as they relate to our major outputs to our customers. We have come to see how technology can streamline access to basic library tasks and processes. Libraries have expanded from the limiting concept of book warehouses to that of service centers which build strong web presences both as a marketing tool and to provide web-based services. As they have done so, their design of technology tools in order to streamline processes and unburden staff is providing for increased customer service as well.

Many manual library processes can be improved by using technology and in turn allow for new and better customer services. While some of these tools have made their way into catalog systems via web interfaces for online searching, there are many other areas in day-to-day library operation that are ripe for the development of technological solutions. David Dorman observes that "Cataloging is being transformed into metadata encoding. Reference is going virtual and is even 24/7 in some institutions. . . . Libraries are creating virtual information environments to augment— and in some cases replace—their physical environments."[6] As community centers, libraries also offer programs and technology training, provide public meeting rooms, and create local databases by collecting obituary and other local information. The processes of signing up for those programs, reserving the meeting rooms, obtaining reference assistance, and locating local-interest data are just a few of the tasks that can be streamlined for staff and patrons alike through technology. Savvy libraries are removing the obstacles to service with the transition to technology for traditionally staff-driven processes. "A second trend is taking place in the traditional appreciation of library tasks as some kind of overhead. This view will soon be completely out of date. In the future, library tasks will be regarded as directly productive forces."[7] As we develop customer-friendly processes and make them accessible around the clock from any point with an Internet connection, we create new roles for patrons in the information chain. Empowered library patrons can now "shop" for services on our websites.

SERVING IN-HOUSE CUSTOMERS

Serving patrons is a deeply rooted element of our mission as libraries. The concept of serving departments within the library as customers is less obvious. As libraries and their constituent departments grow in size and complexity, it is more important to get the tools and processes in place to serve all the customers. The traditional library model is staff-driven. A customer approaches a service point by phone or in person. A reference librarian obtains information in response to a patron query and presents it to the patron; customers approach a circulation desk for checkout or renewal of items; and they request a library staff person to reserve materials or a meeting room for them, or register them for program attendance.

Catalog systems such as Sirsi Corporation's iBistro are making advances as they track item popularity, hot sites, and recommended reading, but they do not cover other common library services. Catalog models do not provide a standard friendly method for tracking such important service statistics as program sign-ups and space reservations. In the traditional library model, the Post-it note still reigns for tallying these processes, second only to the list. Traditionally, if patron-to-staff interaction is required for sign-ups and notifications, a staff member is designated as a "point person" for the assigned task. Those libraries that offer meeting rooms for public use, for instance, generally designate a staff person as the keeper of the list. Libraries that operate as community centers host increasing numbers of programs and events, which require staff time for sign-up maintenance and promotion. Additionally, many libraries make meeting rooms available to the community, which requires staff time for working out the availability of the rooms, as well as a system for scheduling rooms for internal use that will not conflict with outside users. Customers who would like to reserve one of the meeting rooms must make contact with the list-keeper, who also keeps the calendar, and that can require several contact points, hence the harried Post-it notes.

Have you ever been involved in the "hallway hand-off"? You pass the list-keeper in the hallway and say, "Oh, yeah, so-and-so wanted the meeting room Thursday night for a focus group meeting." You feel better. You have moved the item off your desk and out of your mind. The ball is now in the list-keeper's court. (And we wonder how the meeting room gets double-booked!) Then there are those problematic program sign-ups, especially children's programs with their last-minute add-ons . . . or the program that has to be canceled at the last minute, let's see, where's the list, someone who took the reservation failed to get phone numbers, or a couple of names look like they *may* have been crossed out as cancellations . . . whose handwriting does it look like, maybe you can track down the library staffer who took the reservation and get the information that you need. . . . Heaven forbid the list-keeper goes on vacation, or leaves the employ of the library, because orderly room reservation revolves around a single note-book or calendar, which can be anywhere in the library at a given moment. We try to cross-train people, but problems still occur if the main "point person" is absent.

If the details of these scenarios sound at all familiar, you may want to consider adopting a web-enabled database solution. This can facilitate better interdepartmental communication at the same time you are making it easier for your customers to communicate with *you*. It's time to say goodbye to the Post-it note protocol. As libraries grow in both their facil-ities and staff size, many staff members are no longer passing each other in the hallway. Departments and staff who share access or responsibility for data sets are often in opposite ends of the building. The adult pro-grams coordinator and the youth services departments both use the meet-ing and program rooms and need access to an up-to-the-minute schedule, but their offices or office hours may be far distant from each other. In addition, the circulation staff may be taking requests for meeting room bookings from community groups outside the library. This is just one area of information management that is well served by a technology solution.

Better customer service does not always mean just better service to patrons. Departments within the library can be considered "customers" of other departments. As these meeting room scenarios portray, creating bet-ter, easier, and more consistent processes for internal tasks will provide better service to outside customers and internal departments alike.

ACHIEVING BETTER SERVICE THROUGH COMMONALITY OF PROCESS

There is a commonality to many task-based processes that lends them to standardization. This is where process mastering serves the library. As the process is broken down for study into its relevant components, we can identify those that are critical. In looking at redesigning a process for tran-sitioning it to a web-based service, we need to first standardize the meth-ods for completing that process. Part of the problem with paper-based cal-endars, forms, and sign-up sheets is that staff and customers alike tend to complete the same process in different ways. Some will submit incomplete information, while others circumvent critical steps in the process, both of which result in the loss of essential information. It is standardization that makes for easy transition to a web-based service. In the meeting room reservation model, when the sign-up process is moved to the Web, not only is data accessible to patrons and staff simultaneously, but data entry and extraction methods are consistent for both patrons and staff. Similarly, when the calendar or list is transitioned to an electronic plat-form, it becomes accessible to any and all staff that are trained to use it. Standardizing the process through web forms ensures that all of the necessary information will be gathered and reduces loss of data. It also creates new opportunities to gather additional information without adding to the staff's burden.

The transition to the Web effectively adds a 24/7 "point person." As the addition of a web interface makes the process or function accessible to the external customer, that process or function becomes part of "data central." There are many advantages to this. Centralizing data and developing a system for handling the data alleviates many problems. When the system becomes the 24/7 "point person," the automation of manual tasks and the creation of a centralized database lead to enhanced reliability. The data is in one location all of the time; it can be accessed from anywhere in the library; and the method for getting the data in and out is consistent for patrons and staff. More staff members can help patrons, and the burden associated with sign-ups is alleviated. This in turn provides improved patron services, faster response times, more accurate information, and no lost information. The customer has gained greater control and independence, while the library gains improved reliability and better staff communication.

ADDRESSING THE NEEDS OF THE INDIVIDUAL THROUGH CUSTOMIZATION

Technology-based services that supplement day-to-day operations do not eliminate the need for human contact. Maintaining a human connection will always be a critical part of the library's services. Those "local touch" avenues of walk-in or phone-in reservations do not disappear. We are simply adding an additional avenue or path for the patrons to complete certain tasks in a manner more convenient to them. All three avenues still lead to the town square. While many of the services detailed here create a single point of contact for customers, a staff person still must review online requests for acceptance or denial. Staff still make phone calls to deal with various issues such as reminders, cancellations, and program content information. Some library service desks may also deal with fee-based service issues.

The flip side of task standardization is customization. Personalized resources and responses are quickly coming into demand as customers endeavor to manage ever-increasing amounts of information. Amazon.com understood this early on and provided suggestions for new purchases based on customers' purchasing patterns. If you are an Amazon customer on the website, you are greeted by name before the purchase selections are offered, and they are specifically related to items you have previously purchased from Amazon. Unlike some of our library practices, Amazon does not greet you and say, "Here is a list of every item we have added to our database since you last visited our site; have a look and see if there's anything that interests you!" The company knows that you won't wade through all of that data to find the one or two titles that interest you. Instead, Amazon offers a select few items, and if you pursue their links you will be led to a select few more items . . . you get the picture, and Amazon possibly gets the sale. Librarians pride themselves on face-to-face personalized service. They remember one reader who likes westerns and another who likes mysteries, and they point out new materials that may be of individual interest to customers. In the next chapter we will examine the architecture of a "personalized picks" e-mail notification system for new items and programs. With this method, the New Books List of our library business model transitions to a web service built around databases.

Notes

1. "Thus Said," *American Libraries* 33, no. 11 (December 2002): 41.
2. Valarie Zeithaml, *Delivering Quality Service* (New York: Simon and Schuster, 1990).
3. K. Cushing, "Instant Benefits (Instant Messaging)," *Computer Weekly* (18 July 2002): 24.
4. Arar, Yardena, "Starbucks Expands Wireless Internet Offering," *PC World* (21 August 2002).
5. Ray Wilson and Paul Harsin, *Process Mastering: How to Establish and Document the Best Known Way to Do a Job* (New York: Quality Resources, 1998).
6. David Dorman, "Open Source Software and the Intellectual Commons," *American Libraries* 33, no. 11 (December 2002): 51–52.
7. Bas Saveniji and Natalia Grygierczyk, "Libraries without Resources: Towards Personal Collections," *Collection Building* 20, no. 1 (2001): 18.

3 An Automatic E-Mail Notification System

E-mail as a communication tool has become part of our everyday lives. Many businesses have taken e-mail a step further and use it as a marketing and sales tool. Even as far "back" as late 1999 and early 2000, e-mail and the Internet were being utilized in new and different ways. Amazon.com was one business model that particularly intrigued a suburban Indianapolis public library because of the way Amazon helped customers by tracking their preferences and interests. The Mooresville (Indiana) Public Library wondered, "Why can't libraries do the same type of thing?" That is when the idea of an automatic e-mail system for new library materials and programs was born.

HOW THE SERVICE WORKS

The concept found support as a Library Services and Technology Act grant project when it was funded in 2000. The criteria for the grants distributed by the Indiana State Library were that they be used for innovative technology projects that had never been tried in Indiana libraries. The objectives of the Mooresville project were better customer communication and marketing. When board members and administrators of the Mooresville Public Library listened to comments in focus groups, it became clear that their best efforts at marketing and publicity were failing: members of the community still didn't know what the library had to offer. The library needed to reach out beyond traditional marketing methods to grab patrons' attention. The added challenge was to do it in a way that would not burden staff with additional responsibilities. Targeted e-mail was selected as a marketing tool for new programs and services, with the added value of connecting users to those new services through embedded links. An embedded link is a hyperlink in the middle of a line of text. The embedded link in this case would be a link to the library catalog to provide an opportunity for the patron to place a hold on the item of interest.

To begin the project design process, library staff met to review the existing process of notifying patrons about new materials in their areas of interest. They agreed that the process was sometimes patron-driven and sometimes serendipitous. It was patron-driven when patrons requested specific new items or items on specific subjects, which were held for them to pick up after cataloging; it was serendipitous when a staff member noted on the arrival of a new title that so-and-so "might like it because he likes to read World War II literature." The process was by no means standardized.

The existing procedure of publicizing library programs and events was equally challenging. While the library distributed 5,000 copies of three newsletters each month to students in the school corporation, these frequently did not make it into the hands of students in a timely manner. School offices and teachers often did not expedite their distribution, and program attendance suffered as a result. The library maintained several mailing lists for bulk mailings, but the mass mailings were becoming both a staff burden and increasingly expensive as the volume of programming was stepped up. The concept of using automatic targeted e-mails to publicize library events and serve as electronic reminders accomplished the marketing goal while decreasing the staff's burden. No one needed to remember to gather the data regarding upcoming events; nor was it necessary for staff to put together a patron interest list; and best of all, no one needed to remember to notify the patrons.

The wish list for the software development was a team effort by library staff and the software developer. As they worked through the project design process, they identified several criteria for the system to meet. Besides functioning in an automatic manner without staff intervention, the other basic criteria that the system had to meet included the following:

- provide notification of newly cataloged titles
- provide notification of programs and events
- provide the notification in a timely manner
- provide no unsolicited information
- provide for personalization
- provide multipoint accessibility

The patron who wants to read each and every John Grisham novel the minute the library catalogs it is an ideal customer for this product. The automatic e-mail system with its catalog database interface is a model vehicle for the timely notification of newly cataloged items. It is a simple task to build a list of those authors who are most popular in a given library. It is equally simple and straightforward for patrons to make selections from that list. Mooresville created an additional field on the online form for authors whose names did not appear on the pull-down list, so that patrons can type in their favorites.

Patrons can also choose to be notified when items are cataloged on a *subject* that matches their interests. The patron who is interested in new materials on the subjects of gardening or computers, for example, can choose to be notified each time an item that matches those keyword terms is cataloged. A pull-down list of heavily circulated subjects by Dewey classification was developed from an automated circulation report. The most popular subjects comprise the pull-down list. A separate field for patron-entered subject terms was included on the form as well. This kept the pull-down list to a manageable size, but gave the patrons a starting point and suggestions for additional subjects. The system was planned to search the catalog database on keywords rather than just in catalog subject fields. This avoids the problem of matching exact subject terms for the search, when many patrons will use only approximate subject terms.

Many of the parents that we see in our libraries are dedicated to providing a variety of great program experiences for their children. They tell us that they want to know about all of the children's programming opportunities that we offer. Publicizing library programs and events is a critical element of program success, and the automatic e-mail system is an effective tool for targeting specific program audiences. Busy parents who want to get first crack at popular children's programs like Science Camp can elect to be notified in advance of program dates in order to help with their calendar planning. Teen patrons can be alerted to concerts or poetry slams, and senior citizens can elect to be informed about computer classes. The pull-down list of programs and events can include a variety of categories such as genealogy workshops, concerts, summer reading, and book discussion groups.

Individual libraries need to determine how far in advance their patrons need to be notified of programs in order to set the calendar that triggers the automatic e-mails. Timely notification is an important feature of the system. Those Grisham books that our demo patron wants to know about? You can be sure that she wants to know about them as soon as they come in. And program information must be sent in a timely manner to ensure that customers are given enough advance notice to be able to get the event on their personal calendars. If the information arrives too far in advance of the event, they may forget about it. If the information arrives too late, they may already have made other commitments.

People are busy, and library patrons are no exception. They are interested in the most recent library acquisitions, but they don't want to wade through a long list of titles that they don't care about. So another criterion for the automatic e-mail system was that it should provide no unsolicited information. Library staff did not want to become telemarketers. They wanted to go beyond simply mailing a list of recent acquisitions, so that patrons would not have to wade through titles to determine whether any were of interest to them. The idea of "giving 'em what they want"—and *only* what they want, is central to the concept of targeted e-mail.

Many patrons have several favorite authors, or they may be interested in a wide range of nonfiction subjects. The idea of the personalization of library resources was a driving concept behind the grant project. Amazon.com has built an empire on this concept. As customers become busier and the available information span broadens, personalization is a valuable method for managing the information stream. The automatic e-mail web form provides for the easy addition or deletion of authors and subjects to the patron's personal profile.

One advantage of web-based services is their multipoint accessibility for both local and remote users. Because the automatic e-mail system is web-based, customers can access the service from their homes, schools, or offices at any time of the day or night. They don't need to search for their shoes or car keys, nor do they need to dial the phone to find out what's new or what's happening at the library. With an automatic e-mail system, they don't even need to remember to log in to get their updates.

The system as a whole is actually much more elaborate than a simple e-mail program that sends a group of e-mails to customers. The e-mails needed to be generated automatically so no one had to remember to send them. The e-mails had to contain newly cataloged titles or event information, which meant that the system had to search the catalog database for new titles. The e-mails had to be sent in a timely manner, which meant that they had to be scheduled or sent on a timed basis. The e-mails had to contain the information that the customer wanted with no unsolicited information. The system had to provide for personalization, allowing the customer to select the events and books that he was interested in. It didn't make sense to send a list of books or events if the customer was only interested in one item from the list. And finally, the customer interface had to be available from multiple locations: home, work, or in the library.

HOW TO CREATE THE SYSTEM

Creating an automatic e-mail notification system that contains all of the foregoing criteria may seem like an intimidating task. However, by analyzing the criteria, the complete system can be separated into individual pieces. Multipoint accessibility and personalization translate into *web-based forms* that can be accessed by customers anywhere the Internet is available. Since the customer information is personalized and the event information needs to be stored somewhere, a *database* is needed. There also needs to be some way to scan or search for events, search for new books, and *send* e-mails on a timed basis. The library *catalog database* is needed because it contains the book information and what was cataloged on a specific day. *Connecting* to the library database and *searching* for items entered on a specific day are also very important pieces.

The final pieces of the e-mail system are:

- web-based forms which allow customers to create their personalized selection lists and the staff to enter event information
- a local database which stores the selection lists and event information
- a scanner program that contains a timer to check for events and new books on a timed basis and send e-mails
- an interface to the library database that allows a search for items that were cataloged on a specific day
- the library database which contains the catalog information

Ultimately all of the pieces need to work together, but the e-mail system is more manageable when one piece is tackled at a time. Figure 3.1 is a breakdown of the pieces of the e-mail system and how they interconnect.

FIGURE 3.1   E-mail system components

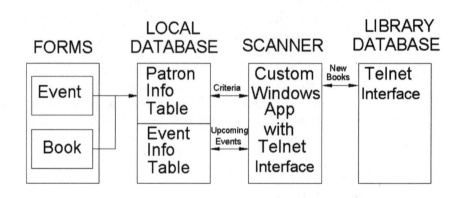

With the exception of the library database, which typically is already in place, the rest of the pieces require some decisions to be made. Again, each piece of the e-mail system can be analyzed individually.

Web-Based Forms

The forms are used to put data into the database and display data from the database. Since they are going to be web-based and interact with a database, a combination of HTML (Hyper Text Markup Language) and some scripting language, or combination of languages, needs to be used.

This is where the decision-making comes in for this piece of the system. There are a variety of scripting languages available (see sidebar). A scripting language is a simple programming language for writing scripts. Scripts are command lists that can be executed without user intervention, that is, automatically. Remember that one of the project goals was for the system to function in an automatic manner without staff intervention. Some of the more common server side scripting languages are ASP (Active Server Pages) using VBScript (Visual Basic Script) or JavaScript, Perl, and PHP. Notice the term "server side scripting." There are two kinds of scripting, server side and client side. Server side scripting is invisible to the web browser, and in turn invisible to the customer. All of the database interaction is handled through the server side scripting, so customers cannot see the connection information and SQL (Structured Query Language) commands to access the database data. Client side scripting is visible to the customer if he views the source code using his browser. Features that need to react to customer input or mouse movements, such as text changing color when the mouse moves over a word, would be added to the client side scripting.

There are a variety of books and websites containing detailed examples and explanations of the different types of scripting. As a general rule, any one scripting language is not necessarily better than another. There are some factors involved that may sway people in one direction or another, however. One factor is the type of operating system that will be used, Windows (NT, 2000, XP) or Linux/Unix. A second factor, in combination with the operating system, is the web server, which in many cases is IIS (Internet Information Server) or Apache. Other types of web servers are also available (see sidebar). Web server software is the application running on the computer that makes all of the web pages on it available on the Internet.[1] A third factor is one's personal comfort level or familiarity with the scripting language. The operating system and web server dictate scripting language options depending on platform.

SCRIPTING LANGUAGES
ASP:
http://www.asp101.com/
http://www.aspin.com/
http://www.4guysfromrolla.com/
JavaScript:
http://javascript.internet.com/
http://www.javascriptcity.com/
Perl:
http://www.perl.com/
http://www.4images.com/ntperl/ (download)
http://perl.about.com/
PHP:
http://www.php.net (download)
http://perl.about.com/

They also determine whether extra software must be installed. There are a variety of combinations that will require different installs. For example, ASP pages will run on a Windows platform with IIS running, and no other software is required. ASP pages will run on a Linux platform with Apache, but an extra software package, such as Sun One ASP (formerly Chilisoft), must be purchased and installed. The same requirement applies for ASP pages running on a Windows platform with any web server except IIS; an extra software package must be purchased and installed. Perl and PHP are open-source scripting languages, so the installs for Windows and Linux are free. The source code of an open-source computer program is free and available to anyone. For the Mooresville project, the operating system and web server configuration was Windows with IIS, so ASP using VBScripting was chosen as the server side scripting language for the automatic e-mail system. The factors in this decision were our personal familiarity with Visual Basic and Visual Basic for Applications (VBA) and the abundance of examples on the Internet.

Once the scripting language was chosen, the web interface functionality needed to be determined. Two key questions determined how the web interface would function. What types of data would be stored in the database? And who would be handling data entry, staff or patrons? The data types were determined to be both newly cataloged item records and such event data as program dates, times, and descriptions. This particular data entry would be handled by library staff. The system needed to permit the staff to enter, modify, and delete event information as well as to control selection menus. However, patron profile information including name, e-mail address, and interest profile data constituted a data set that would be entered by patrons. The system also needed to provide a means for patrons to create their personal selection lists. These two distinct requirements led to a clear division between maintenance pages and patron pages. The staff uses the maintenance interface in which they can enter the pertinent information by filling in predefined forms on web pages. The patrons use a separate interface that allows them to create personal selection lists by using a predefined form. They select from lists that the staff maintain, all of which is keyed off of the patrons' e-mail addresses.

The two most popular web servers are Apache and IIS:

> http://www.apache.org/
>
> http://www.microsoft.com/ windows2000/en/advanced/iis/ default.asp

Another choice is the Sun One Server:

> http://wwws.sun.com/software products/web_srvr/home_web_ srvr.htm

For an annotated listing of web server software packages, see:

> http://www.webserverlist.com/ guides/ServerSoftware.asp

Now that the two primary system components had been determined, the next step was to develop specifications for the maintenance pages and patron pages and the information that was to be captured on each page. The web forms for each page were created after determining the data that needed to be captured or displayed. During development, this can be an iterative process. All of the data is not necessarily obvious at the outset of development. There are generally key pieces of information in hand at the beginning, but as development proceeds, other items are added or it becomes more obvious that they need to be included. It is helpful to outline the key information pieces early in the development process.

Local Database

The next important piece of the system is the local database. The database is the central storage unit, the heart of the system. This is where critical data flows in and out, making the system function. The database stores the patron selections, event schedule information, and miscellaneous support information. The database has to handle multiple connections because more than one person must be able to use the database, the scanner program, and the web pages. Choosing the right database was critical. Oracle would do the job but was not an option because of its cost. The final options were Microsoft Access, Microsoft SQL Server, or MySQL. Any of the three would work, but Microsoft SQL Server and MySQL are better suited for larger database applications. MySQL was chosen because it required less computer resources than Microsoft SQL Server, and many ISPs (Internet service providers) typically offer MySQL as a database option to their customers.

Once the database was chosen, the database structure and tables had to be created. The process of creating the tables works in conjunction with determining the form information since most, if not all, of the information from the forms is stored in table(s) in the database, or information displayed on the forms is derived from data in table(s) in the database.

There are many books and websites that contain information specifically on the subject of relational databases. A relational database is made up of one or more tables. Each table contains separate fields. The fields can also be thought of as the column headings. Data is stored in the table using the associated field name. A basic example of this concept would be if you created a folder or directory on your computer called Contacts. Then, using a spreadsheet program, create a spreadsheet called Phone Number with column headings of "ID," "First Name," "Last Name," and "Phone Number" and save it in the Contacts folder. The Contacts folder would be considered the database, the Phone Number spreadsheet file would be considered the table, and the column headings would be the fields in the table.

The difference between this example and a database program is that the database program contains built-in functionality for quick searching, sorting, and other functions for manipulating several tables. Generally, one of the fields contains a pointer or index into another table that has related data. In other words, the index ties data in multiple tables together. This is important, since searches are much faster on smaller tables. In many cases, it is more advantageous to spread data between multiple tables than to have everything in one big table. Using the previous example, you may want to capture address information along with the phone numbers. Instead of adding all of the fields or columns for "Address," "State," "City," and "Zip" to the Phone Number table, you could create an Address table that contains the fields. The "ID" column in the Phone Number table would contain a unique number for each first name, last name, and phone number. If you add an "ID" column to the Address table and use the same ID value when the address information is entered, then all of the information can be gathered at once. The advantage is that if you are searching by a last name, the data in the Address table does not get included in the search and the search is much faster. With all of that said, it is up to the person laying out the tables and fields to determine when to split data between tables. This task is much easier when all of the required fields are determined as early as possible. Not only is it important for determining the web forms, but it is also critical to the layout of the database structure.

Figure 3.2 is an example of a database structure in which each box is a table and the listed items inside the box are the fields. The lines show how the tables relate to each other.

FIGURE 3.2   Database table relationships

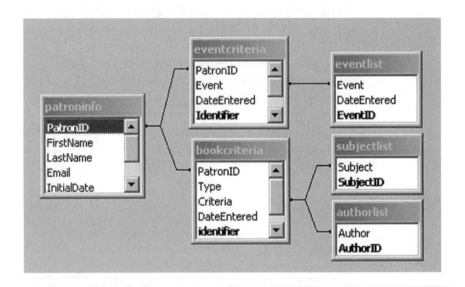

Scanner

The scanner is another critical piece of the system. The scanner is the brain of the system. It is required to accomplish a multitude of functions and keep the system operating. First and foremost, the scanner must run its functions at specific times, which requires either an internal timer or an external program to trigger it. The functions can be divided into two similar but separate sections, event notification and new book notification. The event notification section is more self-contained in that it solely interacts with the local database to determine event information and patron selections. The new book notification section interacts with the local database, but it also utilizes the library database interface which in turn interacts with the library database.

The scanner implementation in the Mooresville project was relatively straightforward, since the functionality was clearly defined. There were a number of functions that the scanner was required to perform. It had to be reliable and it could not require staff intervention. Those requirements steered the development of the scanner toward a single Windows program. Ultimately, a Windows program was created that could run as a regular program on start-up or as an NT Service which allowed it to run in the background on NT, 2000, or now on XP. The creation of the scanner program can require a different skill set than the web programming. However, some of the Windows operating systems come with a scheduler, and there are shareware scheduling programs that allow you to define which programs to run and when to run them. The same functionality could be created using separate pieces of software and a scheduling program.

Library Database Interface

The next critical system piece, the library database interface, was treated as a separate piece of the e-mail system because it required investigation and presented its own set of challenges. In actuality, the library database interface is part of the scanner program. It was the most complex and hair-raising part of the grant project and makes for an interesting story that may provide valuable information for others, so we include the story here.

Library Database

The Mooresville Library's database was Z39.50 compliant. Z39.50 was supposed to be a universal way to connect to a search of a library's database. It made sense to try to use Z39.50 to extract the necessary book data from the library database to use in generating the book e-mails. Prior to the development of the Z39.50 standard, each database vendor had its own proprietary way of extracting data from its database. Using Z39.50 would also permit the e-mail system to work for other libraries that had a database with a Z39.50 interface. That sounded great, but aside from being a buzzword, what was Z39.50? No one involved in the grant project really knew much about it, and there was not much time to do an extensive investigation before the final grant proposal was due. In addition to simply understanding what Z39.50 was about, there were two major questions that begged to be addressed. Would Z39.50 do what the grant development team needed it to do? And was there some Z39.50 software out there that could either work with or as part of the scanner program?

Z39.50: In Layman's Terms

Many websites exist that describe the development and various elements of Z39.50 (see sidebar). That number has grown since January 2000, when the project research was originally performed. Z39.50 is an international standard. The Z39.50-compliant software that comprises our catalog systems is written according to the Z39.50 standard. Version 1 of the standard was implemented in 1988 by the National Information Standards Organization (NISO) as a way for Z39.50 clients (computer systems) to retrieve MARC records from each other (communicate). It is presently maintained by the Library of Congress. Version 2 was developed in 1992. A major weakness of Version 2 was that it did not support the display of holdings information and circulation status. In 1995, Version 3 addressed these issues and expanded support to a wide variety of data types, which should provide for wider implementation and development. Version 3 is the most current version of the standard, and most vendors are now implementing this version. Originally a solution to a library problem, Z39.50 has been modified and enhanced to find expanded use in other communities, including the geospatial, government, and museum communities.

Z39.50 standardizes the search and retrieval functions; in other words, it makes sure that everyone is speaking the same language. As libraries, we benefit from Z39.50 because the standard simplifies and speeds access to collections worldwide, and because it simplifies connecting to collections with different automation systems than the ones we may utilize locally. Z39.50 follows client/server architecture: a computer (client) queries another computer (server). The client and the server first verify that they are speaking the same language. Then the server submits the request and returns an answer. The answer comes in a specified format (MARC, unstructured text). The client can query several

For details on the history and continuing development of Z39.50, see the following resources:

The Bath Profile
Bath Profile Maintenance Agency
http://www.nlc-bnc.ca/bath/bp-current.htm

Library of Congress
Z39.50 Maintenance Agency
http://www.loc.gov/z3950/agency/

Z39.50
BiblioTech Review article
http://www.bibliotech.com/html/z39_50.html

Texas State Library and Archives Commission
Z Texas Project
http://www.tsl.state.tx.us/ld/projects/z3950/index.html

servers at one time. The reason that Z39.50 was important to the automatic e-mail project is because it was necessary to be able to query the local library catalog for newly cataloged items, and a method for talking to the database was needed. Since the catalog was Z39.50 compliant, the Z39.50 protocol was a first choice to access the necessary information.

Z39.50 is designed to create a common method of extracting information from any vendor's database that supports Z39.50. Different vendors that support Z39.50 will have a single *common* way of extracting the same type of information from each database.

A very loose example of what Z39.50 is intended to accomplish can be provided by describing three different restaurants. They are Restaurants A, B, and C. All three restaurants use a numbering system for ordering from the menu and each has the same food items available. Restaurant A is a fast food place where you wait in line to get your food. If you order a Number One you will receive a hamburger, fries, and a drink. Restaurant B is a sit-down place where a server delivers your food. If you order a Number One you receive nuggets, onion rings, and a drink. Restaurant C is a delivery place where the food is delivered to your home. If you order a Number One at Restaurant C, you receive a large pizza.

In our example, there are three different restaurants with different ways of delivering the food. They all have a Number One on the menu, but the resulting food order differs between restaurants. Now imagine that the restaurants do not have menus. You know what you want and you figure they probably have it, but you don't know how to order it. This is an example of three library databases without Z39.50. There is no common method of getting the information that you want or knowing how to get it. Now consider the three restaurants again. They get together and standardize the menu items and make the menus readily available. The items on the revised menus are now identical. You can go into Restaurant A, B, or C, order a Number One, and receive a hamburger, fries, and a drink. That concept may be boring in the restaurant world, but when it comes to searching various databases, it is not so boring. It is very practical to be able to connect to databases in a common way, search the databases in a common manner, and receive the information from those databases in the same way every time.

There are many Z39.50-compliant catalog systems in the library field, so the assumption could be made that there is a comfortable degree of interoperability in data search and retrieval between libraries. In actuality, many other factors cloud the issue of easy data exchange between catalog systems. Z39.50 version compliance, operating systems, and local indexing practices all populate the Z39.50 obstacle course and make interoperability a challenge. A key solution to Z39.50 interoperability issues is conformance to the Bath Profile. The Bath Profile was developed as a result of a meeting of Z39.50 implementers and researchers in Bath, England, in

1999. As catalog software developers implement the Bath Profile in their system designs, interoperability between different vendor systems will improve. Catalog database search results will also improve as a core set of functions and specifications are supported by the catalog vendors as a standard. In the present library environment, most Z39.50 library systems are either Version 2 or Version 3 compliant, with plenty of vendor latitude in attribute subset support. Many catalog systems in the field are not Z39.50 compliant at all, however, further complicating search and retrieval efforts. Adherence to the Bath Profile as a standard will level the playing field. Libraries will have a clear picture of attribute support parameters as Z39.50 compliance evolves to Bath Profile compliance.

Version compliance is an important part of any Z39.50 discussion. "Z39.50 compliant" can mean something different to a cataloger or system administrator than it does to a catalog vendor or to a vendor's sales rep. Version 2 and Version 3 are the important versions of Z39.50. Within each version, however, there is some variance regarding attribute support by catalog vendors. Attributes can be described loosely as features. Another way to think of attribute support is as levels of service supported. When a library purchases a Z39.50-compliant system, it is generally with the assumption that the system will perform all of the necessary functions to ensure that data search and retrieval will proceed in an orderly and satisfactory fashion. While it is not necessary to implement every Z39.50 attribute for this to take place, if the library intends to accomplish local interfacing to its catalog database it is critical that the vendor's attribute support parameters are known. This information is available from catalog vendors as an attribute list.

There are various attribute sets supported under Z39.50, and within each attribute set is a list of "use attributes" that are unique and correspond to various items. The concept is similar to MARC records, where there is a value that represents an item. The attribute set that the Mooresville Library database supported was the Bib-1 Attribute set. Bib-1 is the most widely known attribute set and was designed for bibliographic resources. Information regarding the Bib-1 Attribute set can be found on the Library of Congress website as part of the "Z39.50 Attribute Architecture" section (http://www.loc.gov/Z3950/agency/attarch/). The Bib-1 Attribute set was originally developed for the retrieval of MARC records but now may also be used to retrieve records in other formats.

The Library of Congress (LC) has devoted a portion of its website to Z39.50 for some time. There is also a listing of all the use attributes for the Bib-1 Attribute set on the LC website. For example, "Use Attribute 4" is the title and "Use Attribute 7" is the ISBN number. There is a "Use Attribute 1011" that is defined as "Date/time added to db." That appeared to be the piece that was needed in order to determine which books (items) had been added to the database on a specific day. *Simple!*

The first of the burning Z39.50 questions was answered; Z39.50 should be able to do what the grant team wanted it to do.

The Library of Congress website also provides a listing of both free and commercial Z39.50 software. There are a variety of toolkits for both Windows and Unix operating systems. After reviewing a few of them and testing examples, it was clear that the second Z39.50 question had been addressed: software was available to interface with the scanner program in order to handle the Z39.50 communication.

However, that is not the end of the story. Once the grant was approved and development was under way, the "Use Attribute 1011" did not seem to work. The database vendor was contacted, but a solution was unavailable because, like many other database vendors at the time, the vendor's software only supported a subset of the Bib-1 Attribute list. "Use Attribute 1011" was one of the attributes that was not supported, although the catalog product itself is Z39.50 compliant. The lesson in this situation was that a database that is Z39.50 compliant doesn't necessarily support all of the defined Z39.50 attributes. Now that we had jumped out of the airplane with half a parachute, we had to scramble to find the ripcord for the backup parachute that would still allow us to search the library database for cataloged items that were entered on a specific day. Our backup was to use a Telnet connection and run the database vendor's API (Advanced Program Interface) program that handled the desired search.

Telnet

Telnet is a defined protocol that provides remote terminal access to a host computer. Using the Telnet protocol, one computer (remote computer) can connect to another computer (host computer) over the Internet or a local network. The remote computer can run applications on the host computer as if the operations were being done locally at the host. There are a variety of telnet programs that contain the Telnet protocol and assist in connecting to the host computer. A very simple example is that of one person (remote) calling a second person (host) on the telephone. When the host person answers, the remote person tells the host, in English, that a command is going to be issued. The host acknowledges. The remote person tells the host to sit down and stand up, which the host does. Then the remote person hangs up. The spoken English words are the (Telnet) protocol. The connection is made and the remote person is able to tell the host person what to do. The telephone happens to be the device that assists them in making the connection, but it could have been anything; it could even have been two tin cans and a string tied between them. For most telnet operations, there is a user operating the telnet software and interacting with the remote computer. For the scanner program, there is no user, so the Telnet protocol was built into the program. The scanner is the telnet software that "talks" to the host computer that houses the library catalog. Each database vendor has its own proprietary way of extracting data from its database. Only the specific database vendor knew how to get at the data for the grant project. We were back to using a proprietary method of gathering the data, but it worked and we made a soft landing.

The library database is the critical system piece for the event notification to work successfully. The newly cataloged items' bibliographic information and the dates the items were cataloged are stored in the library database. As we discovered in the previous section, the library database must have some means for searching or querying the data for the date an item was added to the database in order to retrieve the desired information.

Other catalog system vendor databases have been used with the automatic e-mail system since the grant project. Some vendors are using relational databases in which SQL commands can be used to query the database. Some vendors also use the telnet method and their own proprietary programs or macros.

A Return to Push Technology

The grant proposal for the Mooresville project explored the use of push technology to send automatic e-mail notifications based on patrons' personalized selections. About the time the Bath Profile implementers were meeting in 1999, push technology was being hailed as the latest and greatest thing. Its development and deployment suffered, however, both from its predisposition to hog bandwidth and a tendency to overload subscribers with information. The past two years or so have seen a revival of push technology in the development of later and greater web products, among them the concept of automatic e-mail.

There are four types of push technology.[2] Application distributors, which are meant for information technology professionals, automatically send software to users; content aggregators gather information and push it out to users; platform providers provide ways to create content aggregators; and real-time data transfer, an example of which is the ticker that rolls across the monitor. Some examples of push applications include e-mail and electronic discussion lists; online fiction, chapter-by-chapter; the remarkable eBay bidding system, which allows the customer to sign up for automatic bid updates to be sent to her PDA; and the jewel in the crown, Amazon Alerts.

Traditional Internet use is a "pull" technology; *you* go to *it*. The user receives data in response to a query; he types a search string into the search engine and receives a list of resources. Push technology can be thought of as "alternative" Internet use; data is sent or pushed to a personal computer, PDA, or mobile device at regular intervals. *It* comes to *you*. AvantGo is a good example of a push technology. Once you have downloaded the software to your PDA, you may select the websites that you would like updates for, decide how much storage space you would like to allocate to the data, and how many website levels you would like to download. The data will be "pushed" to the PC or mobile device whenever you synch to your desktop or laptop. The significance of push technologies lies in the timeliness of the data that is being distributed as well as their automatic functioning.

ASSEMBLING THE PUZZLE

Once the project pieces were identified and developed, it was time for the system to operate as a complete unit. Since the staff must enter information in order for patrons to use the system, the "staff maintenance pages" are where it all begins. The maintenance pages are predefined web forms that the staff uses to modify data within tables in the database. The predefined maintenance pages eliminate the need for the staff to know anything about databases or HTML. Adding, deleting, and modifying data are as easy as filling out an online form. There are three maintenance pages that the staff use to modify selection list options for the patrons to choose from. Figures 3.3–3.5 are examples of the Event List, Author List, and Subject List Maintenance pages, respectively.

FIGURE 3.3   Event List Maintenance Page

Event List Maintenance

The Event List contains the items that are displayed in the drop-down list on the Event Criteria entry and Event Maintenance web pages.

The first section allows you to ADD an event type. The second section allows you to REMOVE event types.

ADD a new event type to the list:

Enter Event Type: [   ]

[Submit new entry]

REMOVE event types from the list:

MODIFY	EVENT
DEL ☐ Edit	Adult Program
DEL ☐	Children's Program
DEL ☐ Edit	Craft Program
DEL ☐	Family Program
DEL ☐ Edit	Indiana Program
DEL ☐	Young Adult Program

[Delete Item(s)]   [Back to Maintenance Page]

FIGURE 3.4 Author List Maintenance Page

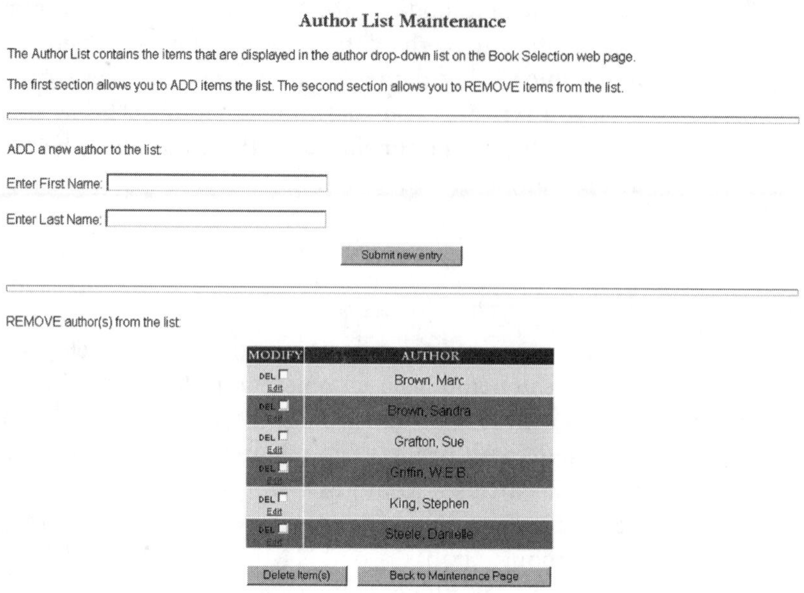

Author List Maintenance

The Author List contains the items that are displayed in the author drop-down list on the Book Selection web page.

The first section allows you to ADD items the list. The second section allows you to REMOVE items from the list.

ADD a new author to the list:

Enter First Name:

Enter Last Name:

Submit new entry

REMOVE author(s) from the list:

MODIFY	AUTHOR
DEL ☐ Edit	Brown, Marc
DEL ☐ Edit	Brown, Sandra
DEL ☐ Edit	Grafton, Sue
DEL ☐ Edit	Griffin, W.E.B.
DEL ☐ Edit	King, Stephen
DEL ☐ Edit	Steele, Danielle

Delete Item(s)   Back to Maintenance Page

FIGURE 3.5 Subject List Maintenance Page

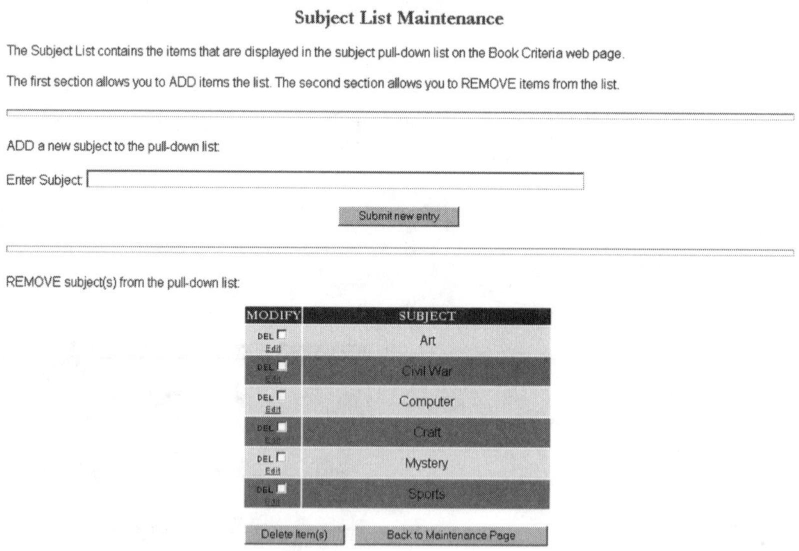

Subject List Maintenance

The Subject List contains the items that are displayed in the subject pull-down list on the Book Criteria web page.

The first section allows you to ADD items the list. The second section allows you to REMOVE items from the list.

ADD a new subject to the pull-down list:

Enter Subject:

Submit new entry

REMOVE subject(s) from the pull-down list:

MODIFY	SUBJECT
DEL ☐ Edit	Art
DEL ☐ Edit	Civil War
DEL ☐ Edit	Computer
DEL ☐ Edit	Craft
DEL ☐ Edit	Mystery
DEL ☐ Edit	Sports

Delete Item(s)   Back to Maintenance Page

The three maintenance pages shown here share the same functionality. They are each built on selection lists. The staff can enter a new item by typing in the item name and submitting it. Items can be deleted by clicking the "DEL" checkbox next to the item and clicking the "Delete Item(s)" button. Editing is similar to adding an item. The "Edit" link is clicked, the text appears in a text box for editing, and the "Submit" button is clicked to save the item. When saved, the list item data is stored into specific tables in the database. As will be seen later, the list items from the tables are then used to populate the corresponding drop-down lists for patron selections. The staff also use the Event List selections when adding an event to the event schedule. This is accomplished by using an Event Schedule Maintenance Page. Figures 3.6 and 3.7 are examples of the Event Schedule Maintenance Page and the New Event Entry Form (the form used to add a new event), respectively. One thing to note is that the New Event Entry Form has multiple uses and contains extra entries for event registration and room scheduling purposes. (They are described in chapters 4 and 5.)

The Event Schedule Maintenance Page lists all of the events that have been entered into the database and allows for adding, deleting, editing, and copying events. The same basic form is used for adding, editing, and copying. It changes slightly depending on which action is required. When

FIGURE 3.6   Event Schedule Maintenance Page

Schedule of Events Maintenance

The Event Schedule contains information on when and what type of events are going to occur.
Use the Modify column to Delete, Edit or Copy events. Use the Add New Event button to add an event to the schedule.

MODIFY	DATE	TIME	EVENT TYPE	EVENT DESCRIPTION	TITLE	SIGNUP	MAX
DEL ☐ Edit Copy	3/1/2003	6:00 PM	Children's Program	Tickle your funny bone every other Monday evening with funny books, songs and finger plays. Theme: Little Bunny	Giggles Gang With Gilmour	YES	20
DEL ☐ Edit Copy	3/2/2003	10:00 AM	Children's Program	Stories, songs and finger plays for the preschooler. Theme: Dogs & Pups	Preschool Storytime	YES	20
DEL ☐ Edit Copy	3/3/2003	3:30 PM	Children's Program	Cool activities, snacks and stories for 5, 6, and 7 year-old bookworms. Club meetings are every other Wednesday afternoon.	Book Worm Book Club	YES	20
DEL ☐ Edit Copy	3/5/2003	1:00 PM	Children's Program	Stories, songs and finger plays for the preschooler. Theme: Dogs & Pups	Preschool Storytime	YES	20
DEL ☐ Edit Copy	3/5/2003	2:30 PM	Children's Program	Words come alive as you have fun with mad libs, poems, riddles, stories and snacks.	Stories & Snacks Club	YES	60
DEL ☐ Edit Copy	3/6/2003	2:00 PM	Children's Program	Create a pebble craft & listen to stories about "Butterflies".	Drop-In Story & Craft	NO	
DEL ☐ Edit Copy	3/6/2003	10:00 AM	Children's Program	Stories, songs, finger plays and the "What's Missing Game" for the active toddler. Theme: Zoos	Time For Tots	YES	20
DEL ☐ Edit Copy	3/8/2003	2:00 PM	Children's Program	Make a Ladybug with book. Please arrive 10 minutes prior to start of program.	Itsy-Bitsy Craft	YES	20
DEL ☐ Edit Copy	3/9/2003	10:00 AM	Children's Program	Stories, songs, finger plays and the "What's Missing Game" for the active toddler. Theme: Zoos	Time For Tots	YES	20

| Delete Checked Event(s) | Add New Event | Back to Maintenance Page |

FIGURE 3.7 New Event Entry Form

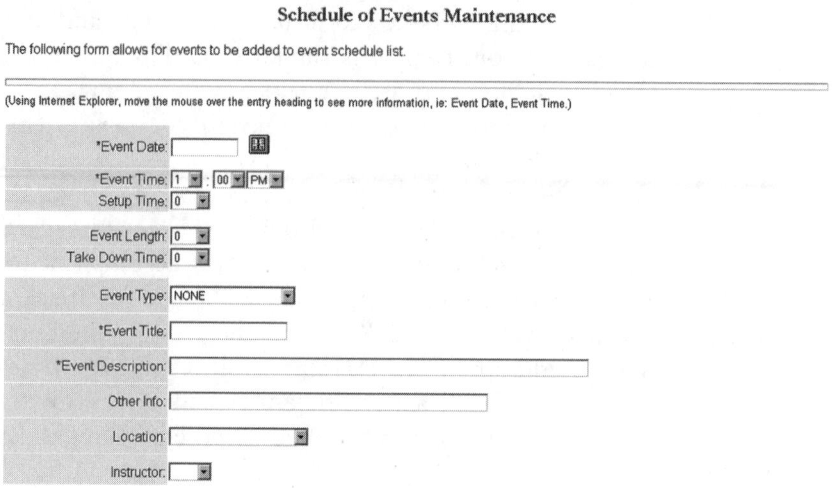

Schedule of Events Maintenance

The following form allows for events to be added to event schedule list.

(Using Internet Explorer, move the mouse over the entry heading to see more information, ie: Event Date, Event Time.)

*Event Date:

*Event Time: 1 : 00 PM
Setup Time: 0

Event Length: 0
Take Down Time: 0

Event Type: NONE

*Event Title:

*Event Description:

Other Info:

Location:

Instructor:

adding, the form is blank and a new event is created when the data is submitted. When editing, the form is populated with the event information for changing and the event is overwritten when the data is submitted. When copying, the form is also populated with the event information for changing but a new event is created when the data is submitted. The key field to making the event notification work is the "event type." The drop-down list for the event type selection contains the list that is created using the Event List Maintenance Page. The event type is selected when the event is added to the schedule. It plays a key role in determining who receives e-mails. The other information (date, time, description, etc.) is used in the body of the e-mail for notifying the patron about the details of a specific event.

There are two primary "umbrella" components to the system, event notification and book notification. Since this is not psychic software, the system relies on the patron to enter information about the types of e-mails he or she wants to receive. This is accomplished through the "patron pages." The First Patron Page is a short form for the patron to fill in and submit. The first entry on this page requires the patron to enter an e-mail address. Everything in the system turns on the e-mail address. The second entry allows the patron to select the category that he is interested in: event notification or book notification. Figure 3.8 is an example of the First Patron Page.

FIGURE 3.8   First Patron Page

Demo Library
Email Notification System

Follow the easy to use instructions and you will receive email notification based on your custom selections.

There are two categories to select from, Events and/or New Books.

Events: You can select an event from a list of events that you would be interested in attending. You will then receive an email notification any time that type of event is scheduled (i.e.: Children's Programs).

New Books: You can select an author or subject of a new book that you would like to be notified about. You will then receive an email notification when a new book matching your criteria is added to the library catalog.

Enter your email address, select the category and then submit the information. Your previous selections will appear along with the options for entering new selections.

To start, enter the follow information:

1) Enter your Email Address: toddc@e-vancedsolutions.com

2) Select Category: Events ⦿ New Books ○

3) Submit the information: Submit   Home

If "Event" was selected as the desired category, then the patron's personal Event Type Selection Page will be displayed. If "New Book" was selected as the desired category, then the patron's personal Book Selection Page will be displayed. Figures 3.9 and 3.10 are examples of the Event Type and Book Selection pages, respectively.

FIGURE 3.9   Event Type Selection Page

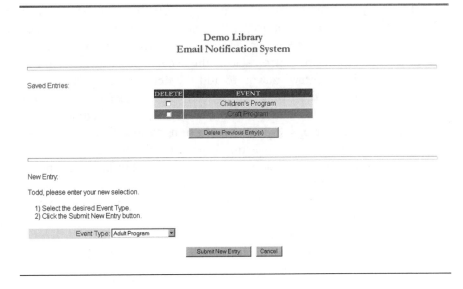

Demo Library
Email Notification System

Saved Entries:

DELETE	EVENT
☐	Children's Program
☐	Craft Program

Delete Previous Entry(s)

New Entry:

Todd, please enter your new selection.

1) Select the desired Event Type.
2) Click the Submit New Entry button.

Event Type: Adult Program ▼

Submit New Entry   Cancel

FIGURE 3.10   Book Selection Page

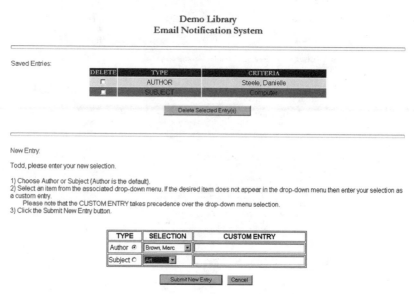

For both pages, the system checks the patron's e-mail address for a match. If a match is not found, then the patron must enter his first name and last name along with his selection. If a match is found, the system retrieves the patron's first name and inserts it into the page text in order to personalize it. The functionality of the pages is also similar. They both display the respective selection lists and allow the patron to add to and delete from the lists.

The major difference between the pages involves the types of items that are contained in the selection lists. The Event Type Selection Page is very straightforward in that the patron has a list of event types to choose from. The patron selects the event type of interest and clicks the "Submit New Entry" button to add the item to his selection. As mentioned previously, the Event Type Selection list is exactly the same list that the staff selects from when adding an event to the schedule. This is how the system ties patrons' event type selections to specific events that are going to occur.

The Book Selection Page is a little more complicated in that the patron can select either an author or a subject of interest. The author and subject lists that the staff created using the maintenance pages are the same author and subject lists from which the patron selects. If the patron does not find an author or subject in the list, he can add a custom author or subject entry. So the process for adding a book selection is that the patron first selects the radio button next to "Author" or "Subject," depending on which selection type he wants to add to his list. The patron then either selects from the corresponding drop-down list or he enters a custom entry. Finally, he clicks the "Submit New Entry" button to save the selection. Like the staff maintenance pages, the patron pages are a controlled way of entering data into specific tables in the database.

So the staff has entered events into the schedule and patrons have created personal lists for events and books in which they are interested. How does that translate into an e-mail? This is where the scanner program comes into play. It contains the "smarts" to know how to use the data that was entered and is now sitting in the database. The scanner program treats event e-mails and book e-mails separately. The times that event notification and book notification run are configurable. In this case, 8:00 p.m. will be used for the event notification and 9:00 p.m. for the book notification. The scanner runs every day at the configured times. This means that the scanner lies dormant and keeps checking the time. It springs into action once it finds a configured time that matches the current time. At 8:00 p.m., the process of checking for event matches begins.

Another configurable parameter is the number of days "ahead" that the scanner should look for upcoming events. For this example we will use 30 days. The scanner checks the event schedule for events that are going to occur 30 days from today's date. It then matches the event types of those events that are going to occur in 30 days to the patrons' Selection Page event types. This results in a list of all of the patrons who are interested in the events that are going to occur 30 days from now. The information contained in each record is pulled from various tables in the database to include first name, last name, e-mail address, event type, event date, event time, and event description. The scanner goes through each record, as long as at least one record exists, and uses the information from the record to formulate and send an e-mail. Note that all of the interaction between the scanner and the database takes place using the local database and the information stored in it.

The book notification side of the scanner is not as straightforward. For book notification, the scanner must have a means to query the library database for data on all items cataloged on a specific day. This requires an extra interaction to take place. The Mooresville grant project required a telnet connection and the vendor's API program to be run in order to gather the necessary data. The way it works is that at the configured time (9:00 p.m.) the scanner connects to the library catalog database using a telnet connection. It runs the API program that resides on the host computer and passes it the necessary information so it will return the author, title, subject, ISBN, and summary information for all of the items cataloged on today's date. The API program would normally send the information to a terminal or a telnet program which would display the information on the screen. In this case, the data that would normally be sent to the screen is captured by the scanner. Since the data sent by the API program is in the same format every time, the scanner was programmed to interpret the book information and store it for use in the comparison searches.

Once the scanner has all of the book information, it runs two comparison searches. The first one is to match the authors in the Patron Selection lists to the authors from the catalog data. The second comparison search was expanded from just a subject search to matching the Patron Subject Selection list items to the subject, title, and summary information from the catalog data. The combined searches create a list of patrons that have matches and require notification. The scanner goes through each record, as long as at least one record exists, and uses the information from the record to formulate and send an e-mail. The e-mail contains such information as the item that resulted in the match, its title, subject, ISBN number, and its description. The e-mail also contains a link to a Holds page (embedded link). In the case of the grant project, it was a link to a page on the library's website that explained how to put a book on hold. The web page contains the link to the actual online catalog system.

One issue that has been a point of interest is that the patron receives a separate e-mail for each book match. The system does not generate a list, nor does it include the list in one e-mail. This was the intended result. The reasoning was that the patron will have an easier time looking through ten separate e-mails and finding the information he wants versus wading through a single e-mail that contains information on ten separate books. Figures 3.11 and 3.12 are examples of Event and Book Notification e-mails, respectively.

The Mooresville Library's automatic e-mail notification system continued to evolve after the LSTA grant project ended. It was given the name "E*notify" and additional features were added. The major enhancements were centered on the e-mail itself. The original system contained canned

FIGURE 3.11   Event Notification e-mail

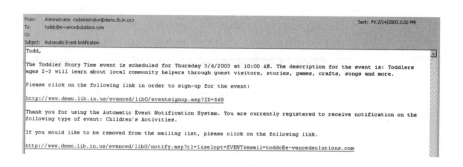

FIGURE 3.12   Book Notification e-mail

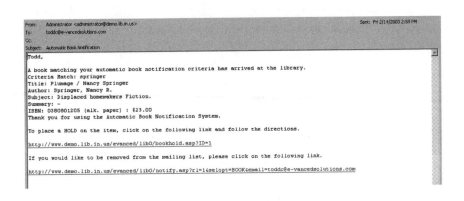

e-mails for event and book notification that were programmed into the scanner. In the enhanced E*notify system, the e-mails were pulled out of the scanner program and maintenance pages were created that allow the staff to customize the e-mails. The maintenance pages look like an e-mail, with a subject line and body text area. The difference is that the maintenance page is used to create an e-mail template. The template contains predefined tags, such as ^DATE^ for event date or ^AUTHOR^ for book author. The system replaces the tag with data from the actual search results. This allows the staff to rearrange the e-mail information and also to add informational or seasonal text, such as "Happy Holidays." A link that patrons could click to and un-register themselves was also added to the e-mails. Figure 3.13 is an example of an e-mail template.

FIGURE 3.13   E-mail template

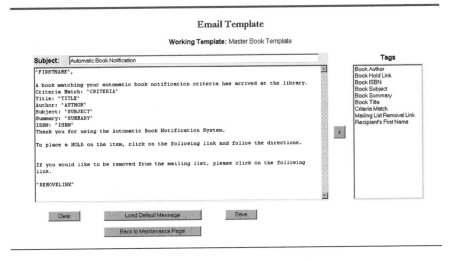

More elements of the event management program were also added to the system. The Event Notification e-mail contains an embedded link to the online registration page for a specific event. Patrons can click the embedded link in the e-mail and go directly to the sign-up page. An Event Registration Reminder Notification was also added to E*notify. This is another automatically generated e-mail that is sent to patrons two or three days before an event is going to occur to remind them that they registered for the event. The online registration, room reservation, summer reading, obituary, and temporary library card systems described in the following chapters use the same database and basic web interface model. They also include patron pages and maintenance pages, like the automatic e-mail system. The next chapter explains the online event registration system in detail.

Notes

1. Definition of "web server software" by webserverlist.com.
2. Leslie Ann Forester, "Push Technology," *Legal Assistant Today* (May/June 1998): 36.

4 A Dynamic Web-Based Event Calendar with Sign-up System

As a community center, the library hosts many programs and events. There are various aspects of event management that affect library staff and patrons alike. From the patrons' perspective, it is necessary to know what events are going to occur. If sign-up is required, they need a way to register for the events. From the staff's perspective, an avenue to market the programs is required, as well as a method to let patrons know what events are coming up. The staff also needs a way to manage the patron registration for events that require sign-up.

WHY AN ONLINE EVENT CALENDAR IS NEEDED

One of the most common ways to let patrons know the event schedule is by utilizing the library website. Many libraries' websites display an event schedule in either list or calendar format. The concept sounds simple enough: the event schedule is posted on the website at least once a month. However, many libraries cannot afford a full-time web developer, so the task falls to one of the staff members. This can be a burdensome task, depending on staff resources and the tools required to generate the schedule. How many times have you visited a website that is supposed to have up-to-date information only to find that the information is one, two, or three months old? The library staff was too busy, or the person in charge of updating the information moved on. Generally, updating the website is a lower priority than other tasks that need to be accomplished inside the library. If updating the schedule is not relatively easy, there is less likelihood of it being maintained. And if the schedule is not maintained, then the information becomes old and stale, which means patrons cannot rely on it.

Creating and maintaining the event schedule on the website is only one aspect of event management. What about events that require registration or sign-up? Not all libraries deal with event sign-up on a regular basis. For the ones that do, this can be a very time-consuming task. Many libraries use paper sign-up sheets and a master binder that houses all of the sign-up sheets for events. The individual in charge of the event has to create a sign-up sheet, find the master binder, file the sign-up sheet in the binder, and let the appropriate people know that the sign-up sheet exists. The patrons and the staff in charge of sign-up then have to locate the master binder in order to accomplish patron sign-up. It may or may not be in its designated location. In fact, the odds are good that it will occasionally be found at the bottom of a stack or on someone's desk. Once the binder is located, the appropriate sign-up sheet has to be located. When that has been accomplished, the patron can register for the program or a staff member can register the patron for it. In the case of a program such as Story Time, which may be offered at various times over multiple days, the patron must get signed up for the correct date and time as well. When it is time for the event to take place, the person in charge has to track down the binder again and find the sign-up sheet. What if he takes the sign-up sheet back to his desk, sets it in a stack of papers, and then isn't around for the event? The person who assumes responsibility for the event has to dig through a stack of papers in the other staffer's office to try to find the sign-up sheet. And that could be one of the better scenarios! The sign-up sheet can also be irretrievably lost. How much staff time is spent in the management and organization of the sheets, including filing them in a binder and finding the binder every time it is needed for event sign-up? How much time is spent by patrons waiting on the phone or at the desk for the binder or the sign-up sheet to be found? When the binder or sign-up sheet has to be hunted down it can be very frustrating and embarrassing for both staff members and patrons. There are better ways to manage the event schedule and registration process in order to make it easier on the staff and patrons.

STATIC EVENT CALENDARS

There are various options available for generating web-based event schedules. One of the lower-tech options that may be considered is utilizing programs that run on a local computer, using staff-generated event information to produce standard HTML pages. These same programs will generally also assist in transferring the HTML pages to the website. There are a range of shareware programs available that can be found on the Internet, and some computer programs also contain this functionality. These programs are helpful in that they assist with the creation of a nice-looking calendar that will work on the website. But they are also limited, since the calendar has to be regenerated and transferred to the website every time a change takes place. These types of web pages would be considered static web pages, where the data on the page is nonchanging because it is encoded along with the HTML code. Another drawback to these types of programs is that usually only one or two people can update the calendar because they are the ones with the software loaded on their computers, and they are the ones who know how to use it. The event information is only updated when the person or persons are available to do it.

DYNAMIC EVENT CALENDARS

A better way to handle the web-based event calendar is to present dynamic event schedule information that is database-driven. The event schedule is controlled by event data in the database rather than being controlled by data that is coded into an HTML page. The event calendar or list is automatically updated and adjusted when the data in the database changes. This is what makes it dynamic. The data in the database can always be changing, and the displayed information changes along with it. Taking library web services to this next level involves a rethinking of their design; designing them less as static collections of HTML pages and more as dynamic resources driven by underlying databases.

Web-Based Calendar Software

A variety of web-based, database-driven, event schedule options are available, depending on the library's resources and the desired operation. There are various websites that host event calendars for free, and there are companies that host them for a yearly fee. EventKeeper and EventTrakker are examples of web-based event calendars that are hosted for an annual fee (see sidebar).

Annual fee-based calendar hosting would be worth considering if a local web server is not available. However, if a web server is available, there are both free and purchased event-calendar software products available that can be loaded onto the web server. The software is generally either a CGI (Common Gateway Interface) or it consists of scripts written in one or more of the web-based scripting languages that are already created and ready to run.

WEB-BASED CALENDAR SOFTWARE

EventKeeper
http://www.eventkeeper.com/

EventTrakker
http://eventtrakker.com/

WebEvent
http://www.webevent.com/

Both fee-based calendars and locally hosted calendars operate on the same basic premise. They provide web pages that permit the user to enter event information. The event information is in turn stored in the database. Finally, web pages display the event data from the database in either calendar format or list format. The user does not have to know HTML or use another program, and anyone with the proper access can add an event to the calendar using a standard Internet browser.

CREATING AN EVENT CALENDAR SYSTEM IN-HOUSE

This may all sound familiar because it is the same method used in the E*notify system, which was described in the previous chapter, for adding events to the schedule for notification purposes. One major element missing from the event-scheduling systems described so far, however, is event sign-up, or registration. As an indirect result of the LSTA grant for the E*notify system, the "E*vents" system was created to display the event information that was already being entered and to handle online event registration. The catalyst behind the project was an attendance problem with selected, expensive library programs and workshops. Some patrons would register for events but subsequently would not attend them and did not notify the library that they would not be there. Many of these events were expensive and popular programs funded by the library endowment, such as Mad Science's Harry Potter Science Camp and the Purdue University mini-archeological dig. The programs had limited space and there was always a waiting list. Consequently, the Mooresville Library was looking for ways to track "no shows" for selected expensive programs without adding an extra burden to the library staff, who were using paper sign-up sheets for event registration. Manual tracking of patron attendance was not really an option.

Since the web page and database support for maintaining the event schedule had already been created for the E*notify system, staff reasoned, why not add support for online registration to it? Let the system handle the sign-up sheets and capture the information in a database. The development process continued with analysis of the paper sign-up sheet process and the information exchange that was involved. The required information was needed to help define the way that the registration tables would be structured in the database. All of the sign-up sheets captured the same basic information: maximum number of attendees, name, phone number, and alternate phone number. Each sign-up sheet also contained any special stipulations for the corresponding event. An example of a special stipulation would be that the attendee must be seven to nine years old to attend. A list of all the possible stipulations was compiled to make sure the system could handle each one. The sign-up sheets also provided for a waiting list, so the system had to duplicate that as well.

One indirect control that is part of the paper sign-up process is that patrons cannot register for an event until the sign-up sheet is available. The staff controlled the availability of the paper sign-up sheet to the patrons. The web-based system allows events to be added to the event schedule as far in advance as desired. So the staff needed a way to set the date when registration would become available for each event. That way events can be added to the calendar one month or even a year in advance, so patrons can see them but they cannot register until the designated date. The problem with permitting patrons to register too far in advance is that they tend to overcommit. This tends to be a problem especially with parents registering children for summer programs too far in advance of the programs.

Once the analysis of the existing paper sign-up process was finished, it was time to add the new features that did not exist before. Additional stipulations were added to the list, and an e-mail address was added to the sign-up information. As mentioned before, the catalyst behind the online registration was tracking "no-shows." A desired feature of the system was the ability to take attendance and have the system automatically "ding" repeat offenders who sign up but do not attend and do not notify the library. The system was to automatically relegate someone who missed three events within a six-month time frame to the waiting list. The person's status would return to normal after a further period of six months. Patrons are notified of their status by a message which appears on the screen after they've submitted their registration request.

Staff Maintenance Pages

After the features and criteria were defined, it was time to determine the operation and the information that would be stored in the database. As with the E*notify system, there was information the staff needed to enter in order for a patron to sign up. This meant that staff maintenance pages were required as well as patron pages. On the staff side of the operation, the staff needed to add the event information, let the system know that the event required a sign-up, let the system know the maximum number of attendees, and let the system know which stipulations were associated with the specific event. The event information was already being entered for the E*notify system, so the existing Event Entry Maintenance Page was expanded. A checkbox was added that signified that the event required a sign-up. A text box was added for entering the maximum number of attendees. A list of all of the optional stipulations was added, along with a checkbox next to each stipulation. The new fields were then added to the event schedule table in the database, so the registration information could be saved along with the event information. Figure 4.1 is an example of this revised Event Entry Maintenance Page.

FIGURE 4.1   Event Entry Maintenance Page

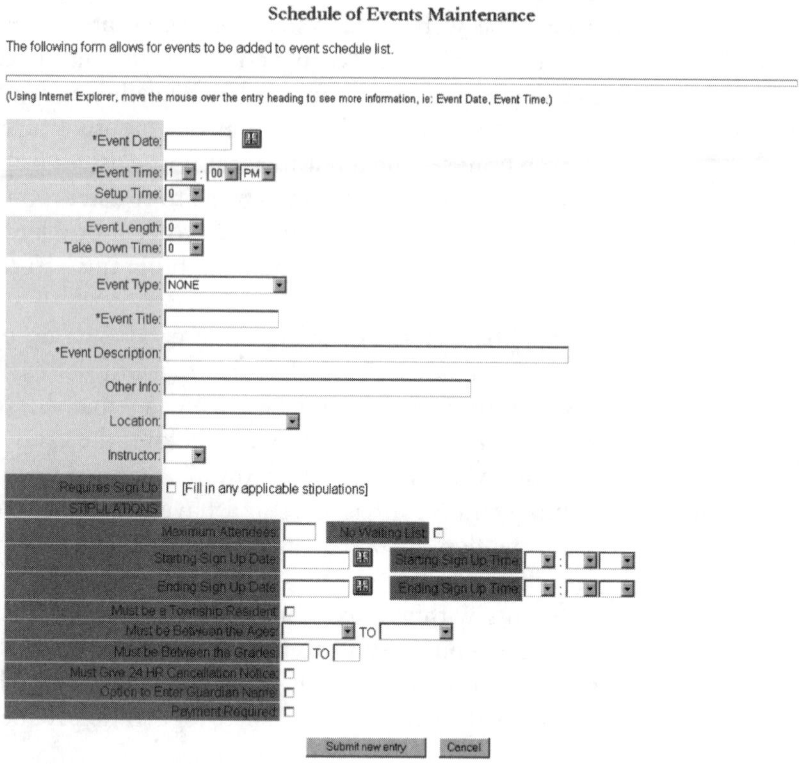

Patron Pages

From the patrons' perspective, there had to be a visual display of the available events that permitted the patron to select an event and sign up for it. The visual display of the event information was in the form of an event calendar and event list. There are many examples on the Internet of displays of data in a calendar format using a combination of the programming language of your choice and HTML. The examples still required modification to work as desired, but they provided the necessary framework to assist in creating the calendar format. The resulting Event Calendar displays the event titles on the corresponding days. For events that require sign-up, the event title is a hyperlink to the corresponding registration form. Figure 4.2 is an example of the Event Calendar. If the event does not require sign-up, the title is displayed for informational purposes only. An example of an event title displayed for informational purposes only would be board meetings.

FIGURE 4.2   Event Calendar

Demo Library
Schedule of Events

Some of the events at the library require sign up prior to the event. The events that require sign up are designated by the underlined event titles. Click on the underlined event title to sign up for the event.
Click on "Display Your Personal Schedule" to see the events for which you are currently signed up.

Display Your Personal Schedule	◄		March 2003	►		Display Your Personal Schedule
Sunday	Monday	Tuesday	Wednesday	Thursday	Friday	Saturday
						1 Giggles Gang With Gilmour
2 Preschool Storytime	**3** Book Worm Book Club	**4**	**5** Preschool Storytime Stories & Snacks Club	**6** Drop-In Story & Craft	**7**	**8** Time For Tots Itsy-Bitsy Craft
9 Time For Tots Book Discussion	**10** Circle Time Story, Movie & Popcorn	**11** Rubber Stamping for Kids	**12** Circle Time Stories & Snacks Club	**13** Bedtime Stories for Little People	**14** "The Roots of American Music"	**15** Giggles Gang With Gilmour
16 Preschool Storytime Iron Man	**17** Circle Time Book Worm Book Club	**18** Eric Carle Collage Part I and Part II	**19** Circle Time Preschool Storytime	**20** Caterer to the Stars	**21** Stories & Snacks Club	**22** Time For Tots Itsy-Bitsy Craft
23 Book Discussion Time For Tots	**24** Circle Time	**25** Babysitting Classes	**26** Circle Time Stories & Snacks Club	**27** Bedtime Stories for Little People	**28** Story Stew: Unending Food!	**29** Giggles Gang With Gilmour
30 Preschool Storytime	**31** Book Worm Book Club					

HOME

Online Sign-up Form

The more challenging undertaking was the creation of the Online Sign-up Form. This form contains standard information: first name, last name, phone number, alternate phone number, and e-mail address. The form also had to contain the proper stipulation entries in order to make sure the patron met the requirements. This meant that a portion of the sign-up form was going to change based on which stipulations were selected by the staff when the event was entered into the schedule. A sign-up form was created that has a fixed area of entry for the standard items that pertained to all events, and which also contains logic to dynamically change a portion of the form depending on which stipulations were selected by the staff when the event was entered. The system was programmed to look at the event schedule information in the database and know how to display the correct type of entry item based on the required stipulations. For example, if the age stipulation was selected, then the form would contain an entry that stated "Enter Attendee Age:" followed by a drop-down list for selecting the attendee's age. The form also checks the start date stipulation to see if the form should even be displayed. If the desired start date that was entered by the staff has not occurred, then a message is displayed showing when the patron can sign up for the event.

Once the Sign-up Form is submitted by a patron, the system checks that the required items are filled out, but more importantly, it checks to see that the attendee meets the required stipulations. If the attendee is required to be between the ages of seven and nine, and "ten" is selected from the drop-down list, the system displays a message that the attendee does not meet the requirements. The sign-up process is halted at this point and registration cannot take place because the required stipulations were not met. Since we have yet to invent an online lie detector, we must rely on an honor system for patrons to provide us with truthful information.

Another function of the Sign-up Form is to determine the level of attendance. Is there an available opening, or must the person be placed on the waiting list? The "Maximum Attendees" entry item on the Event Entry Maintenance Page is used to determine the attendance level. A message is displayed stating the patron's registration status, specifically whether the patron has been registered or placed on a waiting list. The information is then saved into the Registration tables in the database. The Registration tables were created to store the information from the Sign-up Forms and also to link that information to the corresponding event. The system also uses the information in the Registration tables to check that the person is not already signed up for the event that he is attempting to register for. Having the registration information readily available provides for an added feature on the Event Calendar. A "View Your Personal Schedule" link was added to the calendar that, when clicked, permits the patron to enter his name and phone number in order to view a list of all of the events he has signed up for. The idea here is that the list can also be printed and placed on the patron's refrigerator as a reminder. Figure 4.3 is an example of the Sign-up Form.

Attendance Sheet

To recap, the staff can enter event information that permits patrons to register for events. The sign-up information is stored in the database if the patron meets the required stipulations. So how does the staff know who is signed up for what? That data requires another staff maintenance page to display an electronic version of the attendance sheets. The staff needed a way to see all of the available events and then select the specific event in order to see that event's attendance sheet. A portion of this task was already complete because the Event Calendar already displayed all of the available events. The Event Calendar took on the additional function. The only difference between the Attendance Sheet function and the regular Event Calendar function was that the events that required sign-up needed to be linked to the corresponding Attendance Sheet instead of the corresponding Sign-up Form. Extra logic was added to the Event Calendar to allow it to be placed in attendance mode. Once the staff uses a mainte-

FIGURE 4.3   Sign-up Form

Event Sign Up

DATE: 3/3/2003
START TIME: 3:30 PM
END TIME: 4:30 PM
TITLE: Book Worm Book Club
DESCRIPTION: Cool activities, snacks and stories for 5, 6, and 7 year-old bookworms. Club meetings are every other Wednesday afternoon.
OTHER INFO: Sponsored by the Friends of the Library
LOCATION: Children's Activity Room
STATUS: Openings
STIPULATIONS:

- **Attendee Must be Between the Ages of 5 Years and 7 Years old.**
- **Attendee MUST Give 24 HOUR Cancellation Notice to Allow Others on the Waiting List to Attend.**
  (Attendee will automatically be placed on a waiting list if they miss 3 events in 6 months that required 24 hour cancellation notice.)

*Enter Attendee First Name: [   ]
*Enter Attendee Last Name: [   ]
*Enter Attendee Phone Number: (317) [   ]-[   ]
Enter Alternate Phone Number: (   ) [   ]-[   ]
Enter Attendee Email Address: [   ]
Enter Guardian's Name: [   ]
*Enter Attendee Age: [▼]

* = Required Field

[Submit new entry]   [Cancel]

nance page to place the calendar in attendance mode, they can select the desired event which takes them to the Attendance Sheet. As mentioned before, the Registration table contains the sign-up information and also contains a link to the corresponding event. This information is used to display the list of the people who register for a specific event, producing the Attendance Sheet.

The Attendance Sheet displays two lists: the Main list and the Waiting list. They each contain common information that is the same for each event, but they also dynamically change, based on which stipulations were selected when the event was created. For example, if an event requires a 24-hour cancellation notice, checkboxes appear next to each person's name on the Main list. This allows the staff to take attendance and check off the individuals who did not attend and did not give the library the required 24-hour notice.

Another feature of the Attendance Sheet is an option to enter the guardian's name. If that option is selected by the staff when the event is created, a column is added to the Attendance Sheet which contains the guardian's name that was entered on the Sign-up Form. Moreover, the Waiting list has extra checkboxes that allow the staff to move a person from the Waiting list to the Main list in case someone in the Main list cancels or there is an extra opening that becomes available. There is also a provision for deleting someone from the list.

The staff ultimately maintains control of the Attendance Sheets, as it does with the paper sign-up sheets. However, in this case the list is always in one location in a password-protected area and can be accessed from any computer that has a web browser, versus a binder which is sometimes misplaced. Figure 4.4 is an example of an Attendance Sheet that allows the staff to take attendance and also displays the guardian's name. The other columns in the list are standard for all Attendance Sheets.

FIGURE 4.4   Attendance Sheet

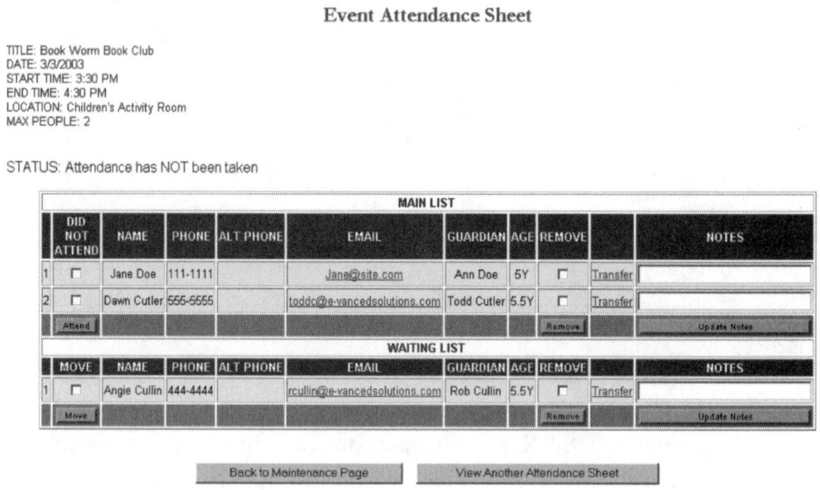

Event Attendance Sheet

TITLE: Book Worm Book Club
DATE: 3/3/2003
START TIME: 3:30 PM
END TIME: 4:30 PM
LOCATION: Children's Activity Room
MAX PEOPLE: 2

STATUS: Attendance has NOT been taken

MAIN LIST

	DID NOT ATTEND	NAME	PHONE	ALT PHONE	EMAIL	GUARDIAN	AGE	REMOVE		NOTES
1	☐	Jane Doe	111-1111		Jane@tsite.com	Ann Doe	5Y	☐	Transfer	
2	☐	Dawn Cutler	555-5555		toddc@e-vancedsolutions.com	Todd Cutler	5.5Y	☐	Transfer	
Attend								Remove		Update Notes

WAITING LIST

	MOVE	NAME	PHONE	ALT PHONE	EMAIL	GUARDIAN	AGE	REMOVE		NOTES
1	☐	Angie Cullin	444-4444		rcullin@e-vancedsolutions.com	Rob Cullin	5.5Y	☐	Transfer	
Move								Remove		Update Notes

Back to Maintenance Page   View Another Attendance Sheet

In-House Registration Maintenance Page

Since not all patrons are going to sign up through the web interface, there was one more staff maintenance page required in order to make the system complete. There had to be a way for the staff to handle in-person and phone registration. While the staff could use the patron interface to sign someone up for an event, a slight variation of the patron interface was developed that provides staff with additional event status information. It is an In-House Registration Maintenance Page. This page puts the Event Calendar in a third mode, In-House Patron sign-up mode. In this mode, the event links on the calendar still take the staff to the corresponding Sign-up Page. Each Sign-up Page contains the same information that the patron uses for signing up. In this case the staff fills out the online form for the patron instead of the patron doing it himself. The difference is that the Sign-up Page contains more information than the patron sees. A section for event status information is displayed that includes the maximum number of attendees allowed, the Main list count, the Waiting list count, and the number of available spaces. This information can be used by the staff member to inform the patron of the status of the event before they go through the sign-up process. Event status information would include the information that there is a waiting list and the patron will be the first one on the list. The In-House Registration Maintenance Page allows the system to continue to provide the same avenues of sign-up that were there before, in person or by phone, and does not eliminate the human interface as a way to register for events.

Additional Features

Since the system's inception, more libraries have provided their input into E*vents and it has been enhanced with more features. One of these features is a Payment Manager, to track payment for programs where patrons are required to fund all or a portion of the program's cost. A "payment required" stipulation was added to the Event Entry Maintenance Page. When it is selected, the system automatically puts the people signing up for an event on a Payment Waiting list. The Payment Waiting list is displayed as a third list, along with the Main list and Waiting list, on the Attendance Sheet. Once the money is received, the staff can move the person from the Payment Waiting list to the Main list. When a person signs up for an event, the system displays a message stating that he is not officially registered until payment is received.

Search capabilities have also been added to the Event Calendar. The same Event Type list that the staff maintains and selects from when adding an event to the schedule is used on the Event Calendar for patrons to select event types that they are interested in. The calendar adjusts to display only the selected event types.

Along the same lines, the system was expanded to handle multiple library branches so that patrons can search events from multiple libraries using one calendar. For example, a patron can search for all children's activities at both Library A and Library B. The Event Calendar will adjust to display only the selected items. The search window slides in from the left side of the screen when the search tab is clicked. This allows for the calendar to use the maximum amount of screen space. The calendar was also enhanced by adding a pop-up window for event information. When someone moves the mouse cursor over an event, a pop-up window appears containing more information about the event, including the sign-up status categories of open, waiting list, full, or payment required.

Enhancements were made to the staff interface as well. Some enhancements were made to the Attendance Sheet so that staff can click on an individual's e-mail address and send the person an e-mail. They can also click a button to send a group e-mail to everyone on the Attendance Sheet who entered an e-mail address when they signed up for an event. More stipulations have also been added to the Event Entry Maintenance Page, such as a "no waiting list" stipulation and the ability to set the ending date and time, which closes the event and does not allow any more people to register after the given date and time. A Location list drop-down menu was also added to the Event Entry Maintenance Page. The list contains rooms or areas in the library where events take place, and the staff selects from the list when an event is added to the schedule. The addition of the Location list necessitated the creation of a Location List Maintenance Page that allows the staff to add, edit, and delete items on the list. The location information was originally developed for display purposes only. However, this Location list led to the creation of a completely new system, as will be discussed in the next chapter.

CONCLUSION

Adding a database-driven event calendar to a library website has many advantages. Whether the calendar software is hosted by a company on its website or the software resides on the library's website, there is no need to know about HTML, databases, or web programming because the systems handle everything. Adding data is as easy as filling out a form. From the staff's perspective, the time-consuming step of creating a calendar and getting it onto the website is completely eliminated. The people who are in charge of the events can easily control the calendar themselves. This keeps the calendar fresh and updated because the changes are instantaneous. From patrons' perspective, the calendar can be trusted because it is up-to-date. It provides a way to view upcoming events anywhere and anytime; this is a tremendous convenience factor.

Going one step further and providing an online registration system adds another set of advantages for both the staff and patrons. For the staff, there are no more paper sign-up sheets and no master binder to deal with. The staff member adding the event to the schedule is creating the sign-up sheet at the same time. The data is in one location and can be accessed from any computer in the library with the single tool of a web browser. In the experience of one library, a staff member was responsible for taking overflow calls from the front desk when the front desk staff was busy. Her desk was at the opposite end of the library from the front desk. She recalled a patron who phoned to register for an event. Prior to the implementation of online sign-up, she would have had to put the patron on hold, walk to the front desk, find the master binder, find the sign-up sheet, and then sign the patron up for the event. Then she could return to her desk. With online sign-up, she used the web browser on her computer to access the staff maintenance page. She clicked the "In-House Sign-up" link, selected the desired event on the calendar, and registered the patron for the event. She was off the phone in minutes. The disadvantages of using the old system of paper sign-up sheets included the time wasted for her to walk all the way across the building, sign the person up, and get back to her desk, as well as the time that the patron had to wait. The advantage of using the online sign-up system was that she was back to doing her work in minutes without leaving her desk and the patron was off the phone in minutes, freeing the library phone line.

The staff members in charge of events have electronic attendance sheets. They can look at a list of names without having to decipher hand-writing and guess a person's name. They can cut and paste from the Attendance Sheet to create name tags, awards, or other items to use in conjunction with the program or event. These are only some of the system's advantages for the staff. From the perspective of the patrons, it is easier to use the Internet than to telephone the library, and it is easier to use a library computer than to ask a staff member to sign them up. They don't have to wait on hold or wait for a staff member to find the binder. Again, it is the convenience factor that is important for the patron; he is able to sign up for himself from work or home, outside of library hours. The patron also gains the ability to check the list at any time or print out the list for reference purposes. The system provides another tool to help patrons remember what they are signed up for so that they attend the event. It can also reduce calls from patrons asking the staff if they are signed up for an event because they cannot remember when the event will occur or whether they registered for it. Ultimately, better customer service is provided to the patron.

5 An Online Meeting Room Reservation System

One popular service that libraries often offer is public use of the library meeting rooms. With meeting space for community groups and organizations in short supply or available only for a steep fee, library meeting rooms are popular places to meet. As libraries grow and expand, they often add additional meeting rooms as part of the expansion. The same meeting rooms are also used for internal library programs and events. When both patrons and staff can use the rooms, there is a better chance that the rooms will be fully utilized. However, as staff members that have to handle the room reservations and bookings already know, it can be a daunting task to manage reservation requests from staff members who are in charge of programs and from patrons who want to use the rooms. Many libraries designate this task to a single staff member. That staffer is the keeper of the master room schedule. If he or she is not available, the rooms cannot be reserved or another staff member must risk making an error on the schedule. This can result in patrons receiving misinformation or being unable to schedule a room because the person who handles the schedule is not available. From the patrons' perspective, that would not be very good customer service.

To the room scheduler, the staff members can also be considered customers. The staff member who wants to reserve a room must go through the scheduler. The staff member either calls or e-mails the scheduler to make the reservation. But in many cases they probably know each other, which can result in a "hallway handoff." You know how it goes: the staff member either hands the scheduler a sticky note or just tells the scheduler his room requirements while they pass in the hall: "Oh by the way, I'll need Room A next Thursday from 8:00 to 10:00." The room scheduler has to remember to write it down on the master schedule when he gets back to his desk or the room is not officially reserved.

WHY AN ONLINE ROOM RESERVATION SYSTEM IS NEEDED

Room scheduling is handled by libraries in a variety of ways. One method is to use a big white board that lists all of the available meeting/program rooms and times. The scheduler writes the reservations in the appropriate room and time slots marked on the board. Another method, similar to the white board, is to use a schedule book that contains the rooms and available times. The scheduler generally keeps the book at his desk and manually tracks the room schedules.

These systems can work for some libraries, but they often result in either the double-booking of a room or in errors being made regarding which room was actually reserved at what particular time and by whom. It must be frustrating for a staff member who has spent hours preparing for an event only to find out that the particular room planned for the program is not available due to a scheduling error. And it is an unpleasant surprise for a patron who reserved a room for a meeting to show up and find that the room she reserved is in use by someone else. Double-bookings are a problem even in some smaller libraries which have only a single meeting room that is available to both the public and the staff for library events. The more frequently the room is used, the greater the chance of a scheduling mistake occurring. As the community grows, so do the odds that the meeting room will be requested more frequently. As the library expands and adds additional meeting rooms, the task of scheduling those multiple rooms is magnified.

The process of making the reservation itself can be time-consuming. Patrons call with their requests, for example, "I need to schedule a room for two weeks from now from 10:00 to 11:00 a.m.," and the request has to be turned into a reservation. Patrons may want to know what types of rooms are available, the times that they are available, their capacities, and the amenities associated with each one. Some libraries post the available rooms, available times, and meeting room policies on their website. This can assist in giving the patron the initial information that he needs. But the patron still needs to work with the scheduler to figure out which room on which particular day and time will work. The patron knows his or her schedule and the room scheduler knows the room availability, but matching the two can be the complicated part. "How about Room A on this date and this time? How about that date at that time? How about Room B on this date and this time? How about . . ." A lot of time can be spent on the phone trying to determine room availability based on given dates and times.

What if the patrons could see the room schedules? Then they could work through the various scheduling options on their own, at their own convenience. Once they determine a room, date, and time, what if they could make a room request online? The scheduler would only have to accept or deny the request and would not have to spend time on the phone working through the scheduling options and filling out the reservation information.

The room-scheduling process can be managed better on the Web than by using a white board or a schedule book. The manual nature of those methods makes them time-intensive and prone to scheduling errors. By using technology to assist in the scheduling process, many of the manual aspects of scheduling can be reduced or eliminated, which in turn reduces the number of scheduling errors. When a database is used to store the scheduling information and a web-based interface is used to manage the data, there are more scheduling options available to patrons and staff. The data is available for everyone involved with the process to visually review the room schedules. The system can help to prevent the double-booking of rooms. By using a common interface, the process is more uniform and makes cross-training easier, so more than one person can be responsible for scheduling rooms. The uniform interface also makes the process more straightforward, so patrons don't receive different answers depending on which library contact person is handling the request. These are only a few of the database's advantages. As we will see, there are others as well.

CREATING AN ONLINE ROOM RESERVATION SYSTEM

Based on the E*vents system that was described in the previous chapter, a room-scheduling system, E*roomreserve, was developed for another Indiana library. Two of the problems this system is designed to solve are (1) providing a way for patrons to view a schedule of the available meeting rooms and (2) allowing them to submit a request online. The idea of using E*vents to help manage library *event* schedules opened the door to the possibility of using the same concept for managing library *meeting room* schedules. The same concepts behind the development of the staff maintenance pages and patron pages could be used. The staff maintenance pages would be necessary for configuring and maintaining the system, and the patron pages would serve as the reservation interface. By analyzing the desired operation for the room reservation system, a basic plan could be formulated on how the overall system could operate for the patron interface. For the purpose of our example, the desired operation is that a patron will be able to review room schedules by selecting a date and selecting a room from a list of available dates and rooms. The patron can then submit a room reservation request by selecting the available times and filling out an online form. There is also one added twist. The patron needs to have the ability to select from a list of available equipment that can be requested along with the room. Depending on the way certain items on the form were filled in, the system will display the correct fee and deposit amounts if needed. After these basic concepts for the system operation have been decided, it is time to convert the concept to reality.

Patron Pages

For the system implementation, it is a matter of taking one page at a time, beginning with the patron interface. The initial patron page must provide a way for the patron to select a date, select a room, and select the desired time. Various conceptual drawings can be created to determine the page layout that is best suited for displaying the necessary information. For the purpose of this example, a final layout includes a small calendar for selecting the date, a drop-down list for selecting the room, and a schedule that displays a day's worth of times in half-hour increments. A Room Information section is also added to the page. The room information corresponds to the selected room and displays the capacity, fixtures, and equipment that are part of the room. Figure 5.1 is an example of the Selection Page.

FIGURE 5.1   Selection Page

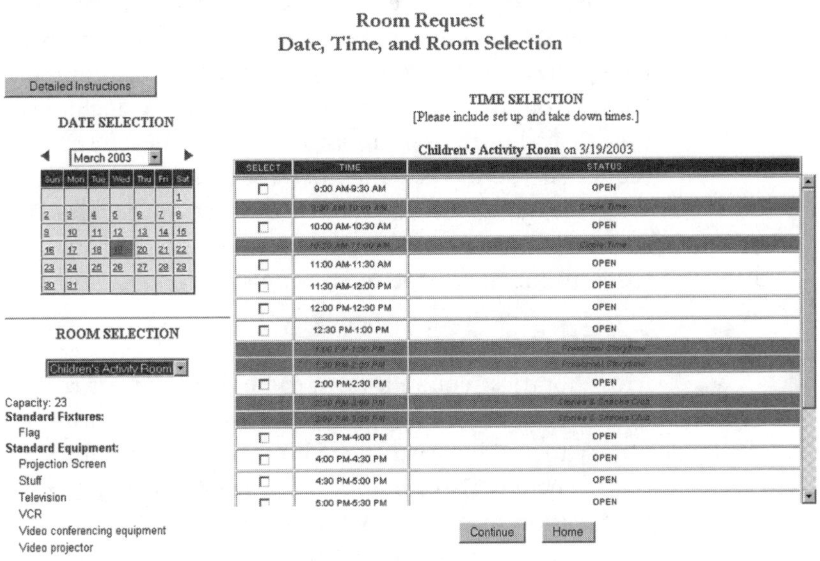

Selection Page

The operation of each element on the Selection Page can be analyzed individually. One of the library meeting room policies underlying our example is that patrons can only reserve a room six months in advance, so the Date Selection calendar is designed to only advance six months from the current month. This limits patrons with regard to the range of dates that they can select from when making a room request. The Room Selection drop-down list is generated from information in a database table. This allows the list to be modified and adjusted without modifying any HTML or programming code, an important requirement in order for the system to be used by many library staffers with varying levels of technical competency. The corresponding room information is also contained within a table in the database, and changes when a room is selected from the drop-down list.

The Room Schedule section of the Selection Page is also generated from data within database tables. The displayed schedule changes whenever a date or room is selected. The schedule shows a snapshot of a day's worth of time in half-hour increments for the selected room on the selected day. The times that are available are displayed as "Open" with a checkbox next to the time. The checkboxes are used for selecting the desired time so that patrons can select times in half-hour increments. The times that are not available are blocked out and do not have checkboxes next to them. This prevents a patron from selecting times that are already booked, and thereby eliminates the possibility of double-booking rooms. The patron selects the desired length of time for his reservation by clicking on the first checkbox corresponding to the desired start time, and then clicking on all of the checkboxes up to and including the desired ending time. This lets the system know which times are to be blocked off for the requested room. As with the paper room reservation system, additional information is necessary once the patron decides on a date, time, and room. A "Continue" button was added to the page for the patron to transition to the next page to continue the request.

Contact Entry Page

Most libraries require a form to be filled out for room reservations. Some of the information or requirements on the forms may vary from one library to another, such as profit or nonprofit requirements and associated costs. There is also common information that is necessary, such as contact information regarding the person making the request. Our library example is no exception. A form is required to be filled out by patrons when requesting a room. In our online room reservation system, the paper form is translated into an online Contact Information Form. However, the online form was expanded to include an additional list of available equipment from which the patron can select. The equipment selections are part of the room request. Figure 5.2 is an example of the Contact Entry Page.

Starting at the top of the form, notice that the identical date, time, and room that were selected on the previous page are displayed next to the

FIGURE 5.2   Contact Entry Page

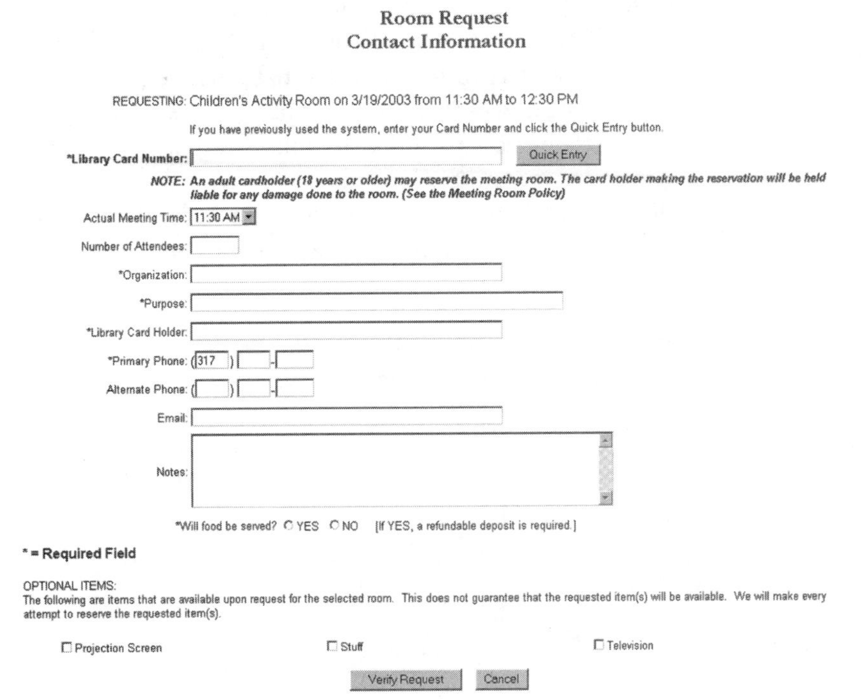

Room Request
Contact Information

REQUESTING: Children's Activity Room on 3/19/2003 from 11:30 AM to 12:30 PM

If you have previously used the system, enter your Card Number and click the Quick Entry button.

*Library Card Number: [   ]   [Quick Entry]

NOTE: *An adult cardholder (18 years or older) may reserve the meeting room. The card holder making the reservation will be held liable for any damage done to the room. (See the Meeting Room Policy)*

Actual Meeting Time: [11:30 AM ▼]

Number of Attendees: [   ]

*Organization: [   ]

*Purpose: [   ]

*Library Card Holder: [   ]

*Primary Phone: ([317]) [   ] - [   ]

Alternate Phone: ([   ]) [   ] - [   ]

Email: [   ]

Notes: [   ]

*Will food be served? ○ YES ○ NO   [If YES, a refundable deposit is required.]

* = Required Field

OPTIONAL ITEMS:
The following are items that are available upon request for the selected room. This does not guarantee that the requested item(s) will be available. We will make every attempt to reserve the requested item(s).

□ Projection Screen   □ Stuff   □ Television

[Verify Request]   [Cancel]

"Requesting" heading. Suppose that a valid library card number is a required field on the form. Since each person making a request can be identified by his or her library card number and since the information is stored in the database, there can be a "Quick Entry" button added to the form. If the person has used the system before, he can enter his library card number and click the "Quick Entry" button. The system will attempt to find his information in the database and fill in the required contact information. Otherwise, the patron can manually fill in his information. The two questions, "Will food be served?" and "Is the organization/purpose non-profit?" have costs associated with them that are directly tied to the answers to those questions. If food is served, there may be a deposit that must be paid before the room is completely reserved. If the organization is for profit, there may be a deposit that must be paid before the room is confirmed as reserved.

Following the questions is an Optional Items section. This section contains a list of available equipment that changes depending on the particular room that is selected. The Equipment list is displayed with checkboxes next to each item. The patron can click the checkbox next to the desired equipment in order to add it to the request. Once the form is completed, a "Submit" button must be clicked in order for the system to check the information for completeness and then save it to the database. Since there is a variety of information that must be entered on the Contact Entry Page, a good way to deal with this is to create an interim page. A "Verify Request" button is added to take the patron to a Summary Page that allows the system to do some preliminary data checking and also permits the patron to review the information before it is saved to the database. Figure 5.3 is an example of a Summary Page.

FIGURE 5.3   Summary Page

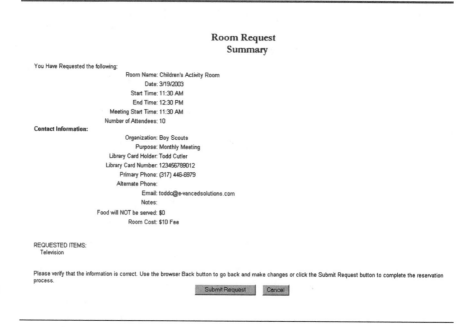

Summary Page

Besides displaying the information that the patron entered and selected, the Summary Page also displays any costs associated with the room. For requests that require a deposit, this particular library has always asked the patron if he would like his deposit check returned or destroyed. That question was integrated into the online system as well and is presented on that library's Summary Page. Once the information is reviewed, the "Submit Request" button is clicked, which saves the information to the database.

A final page is displayed, showing the cost information and where to send the payment if one is required. Following the completion of the process, a room reservation request is sitting in the database.

Maintenance Pages

The patron pages helped to dictate the information necessary to be entered by staff in order for the system to operate. There are some key pieces of information that need to be entered through maintenance pages, however. For example, the first patron page that was described above contains an available room selection list and associated room information that changes, depending on which room is selected from the Selection list. Both items are directly tied to data in the database. The second patron page, the Contact Entry Page, contains the list of available equipment that the patron can request. This page also relies on data in the database in order to display the available equipment for the associated room. The data for both patron pages is controlled through a Room Information Maintenance Page. Figure 5.4 is an example of this page.

FIGURE 5.4   Room Information Maintenance Page

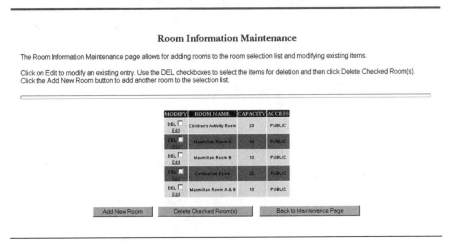

Add New Room Page

The Room Information Maintenance Page is used to display how individual rooms are configured and to allow the staff to add, edit, and delete rooms. The "Add" and "Edit" options are used to configure a new room or make changes to an existing room. An online form, the Add New Room Page, is used to add new rooms that are available for reservation. This same form is used for adding and editing a room reservation. When

"Add" is selected, the form appears blank and with any defaults set. When "Edit" is selected, the form appears with the information filled in according to how the room was previously configured.

The Add New Room Page is divided into four sections. They are Room Display Information, Contact Entry Items, Room Costs, and Room Availability. Since the form as a whole contains quite a bit of information, each section of the form will be broken down and described below.

Room Display Section   The Room Display section contains the room information that is displayed and the schedule operation that takes place on the first patron page—i.e., the Selection Page. Figure 5.5 is an example of the Room Display section on the Add New Room Page.

As described in the previous chapter, E*vents contains a Location list that is a master list of all rooms. The same list is used for configuring rooms that are available for reserving. The Select Room drop-down list in the Room Display section is a list of rooms that are eligible to be configured. This list is generated by taking all of the room names configured in the Location list and subtracting those room names that have already been configured as available rooms. The room that is selected from the list is the room that is subsequently configured using the rest of the form.

Also available within the Room Display section is the "Accessibility" entry. This option was not part of the original project conception. As described previously, the Selection Page displays the schedule of a specific room with checkboxes next to the available times. The patron uses the checkboxes to select the times that he or she is interested in. Some questions arose. What if the library wants to still control a room and allow the

FIGURE 5.5   Room Display section of Add New Room Page

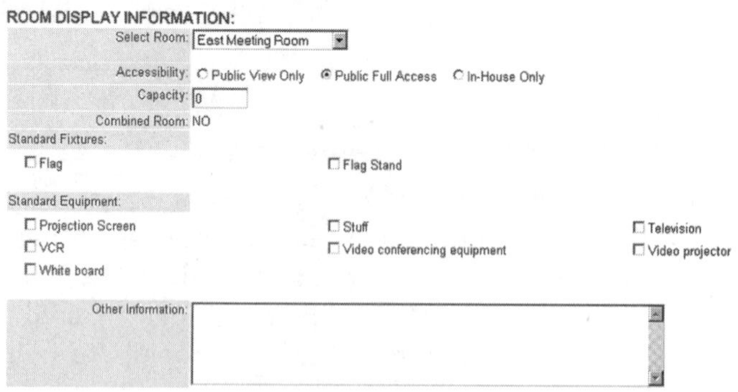

patron to look at the room's availability but not request a reservation? What if the room is only available internally for reservation and patrons should not even see its availability, such as a conference room? These questions were answered by adding the "Accessibility" option. This gives the staff the ability to set the room as one of three options, "Public View Only," "Public Full Access," and "In-House Only." "Public View Only" allows the patron to see the schedule but not make a request; the "Time Selection" checkboxes do not appear. "Public Full Access" allows the patron to see the schedule and make requests. "In-House Only" makes the room invisible to patrons. Only staff members can see the room and reserve it through a special maintenance page, which is discussed in a later section of this chapter.

There are also lists of standard fixtures and of standard equipment available in the Room Display section. The information for the Fixture and Equipment lists is contained in tables in the database. The Standard Fixture list is maintained through a Fixture List Maintenance Page. The Standard Equipment list is maintained through an Equipment List Maintenance Page. These two maintenance pages are identical in operation and are used so the staff can add, edit, and delete fixtures and equipment on the lists. The lists serve as master lists of all the possible fixtures and equipment that can be selected for any room. The list items are displayed on the form with checkboxes next to each item. The items are selected when a room is configured, which ties the fixtures and equipment with the given room being configured. This is the standard information that the patron sees when a room is selected on the first patron page. The term "standard" is used because the fixtures or equipment are part of the room.

Contact Entry Items Section   The next section, Contact Entry Items, contains items that affect the Contact Entry Page. Figure 5.6 is an example of the items in the Contact Items section that are available for configuring how the Contact Entry Page looks and acts when a room is being requested.

FIGURE 5.6   Contact Entry Items section of Add New Room Page

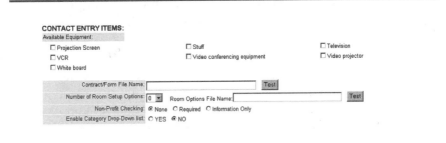

The first item is an Available Equipment list. This list is the exact same list as the Standard Equipment list and is displayed in the same manner, with checkboxes next to each item. The only difference between the lists is how the system utilizes the two lists. The Standard Equipment list is for fixed equipment, or equipment that is always part of the room, and is displayed on the first patron page. The Available Equipment list is for equipment that can be moved into the room upon request. The available equipment items that are configured for a given room appear on the Contact Entry Page for patrons to select when the given room is requested.

The other items in the Contact Entry Items section were added for other libraries that had varying contact entry forms. The items are "Contract/Form File Name," "Number of Room Setup Options," "Non-Profit Checking," and "Enable Category Drop-Down List." They determine which entry items are displayed on the Contact Entry Page. If the "Contract/Form File Name" item contains a path to a web page or image, then an entry item appears on the Contact Entry Page stating "A contract must accompany the reservation," with a button that displays the Contract Page or image and allows the patron to print it out. Some libraries have a field on their paper forms that allows the patron to select a room configuration from a graphic of the available room configuration options, such as classroom or lecture seating. That same entry item appears on the Contact Entry Page if the "Number of Room Setup Options" item is configured. It is configured by selecting the number of options that the patron can choose from and entering a path to a web page or image file that contains the graphics for the configuration options. The Contact Entry Page then displays an entry item for room setup that has selections for an alphabetical sequence of the options that were configured. Next to it, a "View Room Setup Options" button appears that, when clicked, displays the graphics for the available options. For example, if "3" was selected for the number of room setup options, the Contact Entry Page will display selection options A, B, and C. When the "View Room Setup Options" button is clicked, a window will pop up displaying a graphic representation of what options A, B, and C represent.

The "Non-Profit Checking" selection in the Contact Entry Items section can take on various uses, depending on the library's policies. There are some libraries that only allow nonprofit organizations to reserve rooms. Other libraries do not require that an organization be nonprofit, but they want to track the number of reservations by both nonprofit and for-profit groups. The "Non-Profit Checking" item handles both scenarios. The configuration options are "None," "Required," and "Information Only." If either the "Required" or "Information Only" options are selected, a question appears on the Contact Entry form asking if the organization is nonprofit. The system response differs, depending on the user's answer to this question. For example, if the room is configured with the "Required" option selected, the system will not let the patron complete the room request if he answers "No" in response to the question of whether the organization is nonprofit. If the room is configured with the "Information Only" option selected, the system will save the data on the organization's for-profit or nonprofit status. If the "None" option is selected, the non-profit checking is disabled on the Contact Entry form.

The "Enable Category Drop-Down List" selection is used to display a drop-down list of categories or types of organizations, such as Scouts, to appear on the Contact Entry Page. The patron can select from these when making a room request. This information is another way for the library to track room requests. As with all flexible lists in the system, a Category Maintenance Page was created to allow the staff to control the drop-down list.

Room Costs Section   The fee requirement issues for a given room are configured in the Room Costs section. Figure 5.7 shows the options that are used to configure the costs for a given room.

FIGURE 5.7   Room Costs section of Add New Room Page

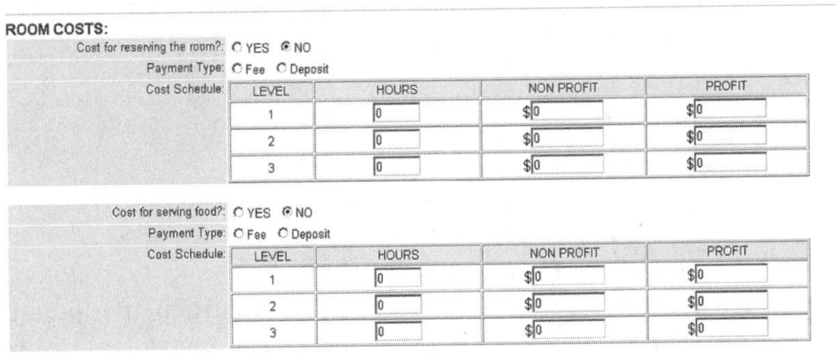

There are various ways that libraries handle costs for reserving rooms. Some libraries charge a flat fee no matter who is reserving the room. Others charge a sliding fee based on the organization's for-profit or non-profit status or based on the number of hours the room is used. Some libraries charge a nonrefundable fee, while others only require a refundable deposit. Then there are food issues. Some libraries do not allow food, while others permit food only with the payment of an associated fee or deposit. The "Cost for Reserving a Room" checkbox must be checked in order to let the system know that there are costs involved when a patron requests a room. The system also needs to know whether the payment type is fee-based or deposit-based, because that affects how the costs are calculated and displayed to the patron when she makes a request. The same information is configured for the costs associated with serving food. Once the cost schedule is configured for the given room, the system uses it to calculate the fee and deposit costs based on the input from the Contact Information Page. If there is a variance between the nonprofit and for-profit amounts, a question appears on the Contact Entry Page asking whether the organization is nonprofit.

Room Availability Section   The Room Availability section is the last section that can be configured on the Add New Room Page. As shown in figure 5.8, the section contains drop-down lists for configuring start and end times for each day of the week.

This section was added after the original room reservation system was completed. The original system contained one start-time and one end-time

FIGURE 5.8   Room Availability section of Add New Room Page

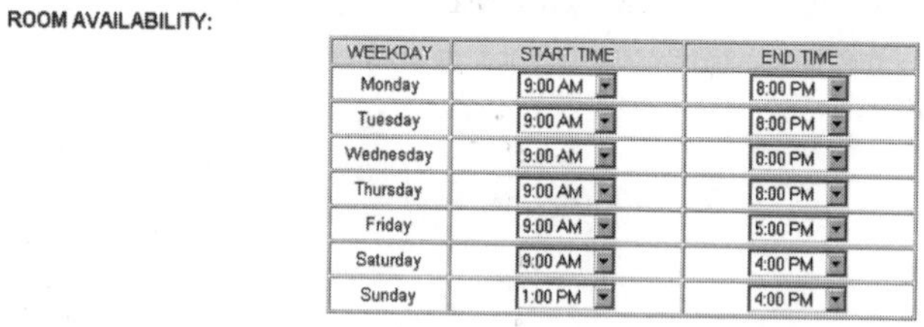

ROOM AVAILABILITY:

WEEKDAY	START TIME	END TIME
Monday	9:00 AM	8:00 PM
Tuesday	9:00 AM	8:00 PM
Wednesday	9:00 AM	8:00 PM
Thursday	9:00 AM	8:00 PM
Friday	9:00 AM	5:00 PM
Saturday	9:00 AM	4:00 PM
Sunday	1:00 PM	4:00 PM

for all rooms on all days. That arrangement did not accurately fit the reality of the situation. There may be particular rooms that are available at certain times when other rooms are unavailable, such as a room that is used by the staff in the morning for Story Time, but is available during the afternoon. Some rooms may only be available on certain days. These types of requirements required a modification to the system to allow per room scheduling of available days and times. The days and times that are configured for the given room affect the room's daily schedule that is displayed on the first patron page. For example, Room A is configured to be available from 8:00 a.m. to 9:00 p.m. on Monday. Room B is configured for 10:00 a.m. to 6:00 p.m. on Monday. When a patron starts to make a reservation and selects a date that is on a Monday and selects Room A from the room list, a schedule will be displayed for Room A that starts at 8:00 a.m. and ends at 9:00 p.m. If the patron selects Room B for the same date, then the schedule for Room B will be displayed with a starting time of 10:00 a.m. and an ending time of 6:00 p.m. This limits the available reservation time to between the configured starting and ending times for a given room on the selected day.

After all the sections in the Add New Room Page are filled out, the "Submit New Entry" button is clicked to check the information and save it in the database. To bring the room configuration pieces together, Fixture List, Equipment List, and Location List Maintenance pages were created to maintain the associated master list of selection items for all rooms. A room maintenance interface was created to configure information that pertained to each room. The master lists are then used on the Add New Room and Edit Room Maintenance pages as options available for configuring a single room. The options that pertain to the room are selected, along with the other configuration options that have been described. Once the room is configured, the information is saved in the database. The saved configuration information is then used by the patron interface to display the room information and proper entry form items, depending on the room and date selected by the patron. The patron completes the room request information and submits it. If the system accepts the information, then the request is saved in the database.

Room Request Maintenance Pages

In order to complete the reservation process, the staff needed a way to review the room requests and accept or deny them. The room requests that are saved in the database are still just requests. On the first patron page (the Selection Page), the time is blocked out on the room schedule and the word "[Pending]" appears next to the organization's name. The staff ultimately decides whether the request becomes a reservation. The Room Request Maintenance Page was created for viewing, accepting, and denying room requests. The page contains two sections, Pending Room Requests and Pending Payments. All requests start on the Pending Room Requests list. Figure 5.9 is an example of the Room Request Maintenance Page that contains both pending requests and pending payments.

FIGURE 5.9   Room Request Maintenance Page

Room Request Maintenance

PENDING ROOM REQUESTS

DELETE		REQUESTED ON	ROOM NAME	REQUEST DATE	START TIME	END TIME	ORGANIZATION
☐	VIEW	2/16/2003	Children's Activity Room	Wednesday, March 19, 2003	11:30 AM	12:30 PM	Boy Scouts

Delete   Back to Maintenance Page

PENDING PAYMENTS AS OF 2/16/2003

DELETE		REQUESTED ON	ROOM NAME	REQUEST DATE	START TIME	END TIME	ORGANIZATION
☐	VIEW	1/30/2003	Children's Activity Room	Thursday, January 02, 2003	9:00 AM	9:30 AM	Test
☐	VIEW	1/30/2003	Macmillan Room A	Thursday, January 30, 2003	9:00 AM	9:30 AM	Test

Delete   Back to Maintenance Page

The Pending Room Requests section displays a list of pending room requests, starting with the oldest request at the top and ending with the most recent request at the bottom. As shown in the figure, the list contains basic information about the request along with options for deleting and viewing a request. The "View" link takes the staff to a View Room Request Maintenance Page that allows them to view the request and contact information that was entered for the room request. Figure 5.10 is an example of the information displayed on the View Room Request Maintenance Page.

FIGURE 5.10   View Room Request Maintenance Page

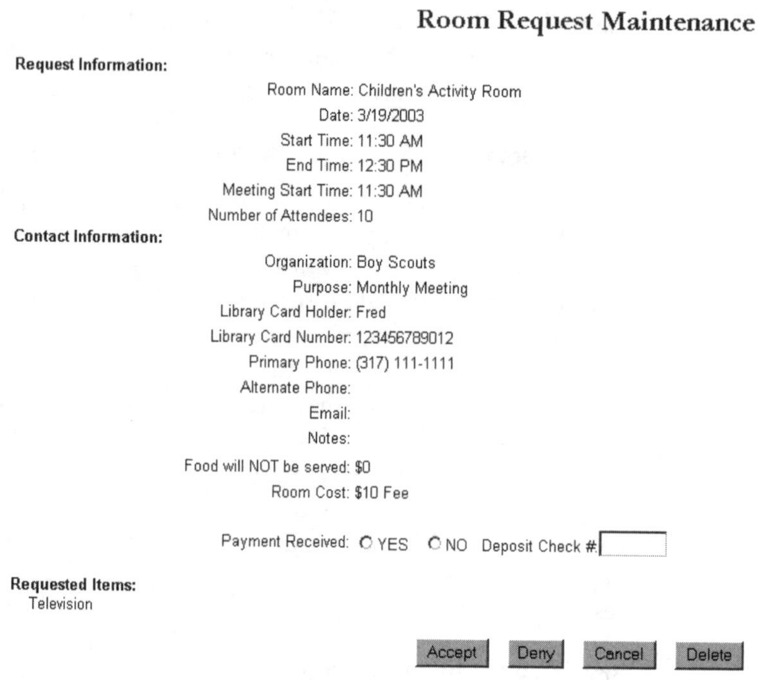

Room Request Maintenance

Request Information:

Room Name: Children's Activity Room
Date: 3/19/2003
Start Time: 11:30 AM
End Time: 12:30 PM
Meeting Start Time: 11:30 AM
Number of Attendees: 10

Contact Information:

Organization: Boy Scouts
Purpose: Monthly Meeting
Library Card Holder: Fred
Library Card Number: 123456789012
Primary Phone: (317) 111-1111
Alternate Phone:
Email:
Notes:
Food will NOT be served: $0
Room Cost: $10 Fee

Payment Received: ○ YES   ○ NO   Deposit Check #

Requested Items:
Television

[Accept]   [Deny]   [Cancel]   [Delete]

The staff can review the information and accept or deny the request. They can also delete the request from this page. As mentioned previously, all requests start on the Pending Room Requests list. The request can be sent a few different directions depending on whether the request is accepted and whether payment is required or not. In any case, if the request is denied, then another page is displayed that asks the staff member whether the contact person, or requester, has been contacted. If the staff member answers "Yes," the reservation is deleted from the system. If the staff member answers "No," the reservation remains on the Pending Room Requests list, displayed in italics, until the contact is notified. If payment is not required and the request is accepted, the room is reserved. As shown in the figure, if payment is required, an option appears for entering whether or not payment was received for the specific request. The staff must answer this question before accepting or denying the request. If payment is received and the request is accepted, the room is reserved. Otherwise, if the payment is not received and the request is accepted, the request goes to the Pending Payments list. A patron can use a library computer, submit a request, and have the request accepted and paid for at one time. The other option allows for the patron to submit a room request, wait for the staff to accept the request, and then pay for the room. This makes for a two-step process, but it ensures that the reservation is accepted before the patron must make a payment.

Pending Payments Section   The Pending Payments list on the Room Request Maintenance Page is similar to the Pending Room Requests list in that it contains the same columns and options. The difference is that the Pending Payments list contains the requests that have been accepted but still require payment. The staff can view the request, which takes them to the same View Room Request Page shown in figure 5.10. The only difference is that the "Accept" and "Deny" buttons are replaced by a "Submit" button. A staff member can select whether payment has been received. If "Yes" is selected for the "Payment Received" entry and the "Submit" button is clicked, the request becomes a reservation. If not, the request stays on the Pending Payments list.

View All Patron Reservations Page

The request does not disappear once it becomes a reservation. The staff still needs to have the ability to see a list of reservations and view a specific reservation if necessary. The View All Patron Reservations Maintenance Page was created for that purpose. The staff can display a list of all room reservations or display a list of room reservations for a given day. The list can be sorted by "Room Name," "Reservation Date," "Start Time," and "Organization." The staff can delete, view, edit, and copy any reservation that is on the list.

In-House Room Reservation Mode

As mentioned in the discussion of the Room Display section of the Add New Room Page, the "Accessibility" option gives the staff the ability to set the room as "Public View Only," "Public Full Access," and "In-House Only." "Public View Only" allows the patron to see the schedule but not make a request. The time selection checkboxes are not available to the patron. "In-House Only" makes the room invisible to patrons. The staff needed a way to reserve rooms that were configured as "Public View Only" and "In-House Only." A new maintenance page was not necessary for this. The patron interface pages were used and some extra logic was added to allow the patron pages to be put into an In-House Room Reservation mode. When in this mode, all room schedules contain time selection checkboxes regardless of how the room is configured, and the room selection drop-down list expands to include all configured rooms, both public and in-house. The rooms that are configured as "Public View Only" can be reserved, since the time selection checkboxes are available. This allows the staff to control the reservations for certain rooms. Patrons can see the schedule, but they still have to personally make the reservation. The staff uses this mode of operation when the patron wants to make a reservation for a "Public View Only" room. The expanded selection list allows all rooms, including the in-house rooms, to be selected and requested using the same process that patrons use for other room requests, with one exception. Since only a staff member can enter a request in this mode, the request bypasses the Pending Requests list. It is understood that once the request is completed it is automatically accepted. Otherwise the staff member would not complete the request. This mode of operation also allows the staff to view and reserve rooms that are not available to the public, such as conference rooms.

Requested Equipment Page

As previously described, the Contact Entry Page contains a section that provides for equipment to be requested at the same time that the room request is made. A Requested Equipment Maintenance Page was created so that a list of either all equipment requests or a single day of equipment requests can be viewed. The list can also be sorted by "Room Name," "Reserve Date," "Start Time," "Equipment," or "Organization." This permits the staff who are in charge of the equipment to review the list whenever so desired in order to verify that the equipment is in the correct room at the correct time.

The original online room reservation system contains all of the elements in the paper or white-board room reservation system, along with additional capabilities. As a stand-alone system it works very well. However, the library that was originally going to use the room reservation system was also using E*vents. Before the room reservation system was completed, it became obvious that when the two systems were used in tandem, additional capabilities would need to be added.

COORDINATING THE ROOM RESERVATION SYSTEM
WITH THE EVENT CALENDAR SYSTEM

The way the original room reservation system was designed, any event or patron activity that required a room had to go through the reservation system in order for the rooms to be properly scheduled. As described in the previous chapter, E*vents contains a Location list that is a master list of all rooms. The Location list is used in E*vents to select a room whenever adding or editing an event. The same list is used for configuring rooms on the Add New Room Page. So a staff member had to add an event to the event schedule system and select the room and times that the event was going to occur. Then she had to go to the room reservation system and fill in the same information in order to reserve the room. If she did not take that last step, she had to notify the person responsible for the reservation system so that person could enter the reservation. If too much time elapsed between the addition of the event to the event schedule and the reservation of the necessary room in the room reservation system, there was always the chance that another staff member might reserve the same room at the same time, causing the dreaded double-booking to occur. The solution to this problem was to make the room reservation system smart enough to look at the event schedule in order to block out redundant events and patron reservations for a given room.

Maintenance Pages

The room reservation system was expanded to look at the event schedule database (which is maintained through the E*vents system) whenever a patron chooses to make a room request. Event reservations are displayed differently from patron reservations in order to distinguish between the two. When the patron selects a date and room, the Room Schedule section of the Selection Page shows all blocked or unavailable times for both event reservations and patron reservations.

The process had to actually go in the other direction in order for a conflict-checking function to be added to E*vents. It looks at the event schedule and room reservation tables in the databases and checks for conflicts between their dates, times, and locations before the event is added to the database. If a conflict exists, the staff member is shown the entry that caused the conflict and the event is not added to the schedule. The staff member can go back and change event information. If no conflicts exist, the event is added to the schedule and the room is reserved for the event.

View All Reservations Pages

When using E*vents for scheduling rooms along with the room reservation system, another maintenance page was necessary to display a combined schedule. The View All Patron Reservations Maintenance Page displays the reservations that were entered using the room reservation system. A View All Reservations Maintenance Page was also created to display a combined list of all room reservations. This allows the staff to see a list of all reservations or a day's worth of reservations for both internal events and patron activities.

Combined Room Scheduling

The room reservation system was further enhanced after the system had been in use for a period of time. Many libraries have meeting rooms that can be partitioned or expanded by using removable walls. This means that they can have a Room A, Room B, or Room A + B. The original system could not handle the ability to create and reserve combined rooms. This functionality was added so that the staff could configure a combined room from two or more single rooms. The patron pages then recognize that a room is either *part* of a combined room or *is* the combined room. The first patron page—the Selection Page—adjusts to display a room schedule that reflects the combined room schedule.

There are two ways that a combined room schedule is handled. If the actual combined room is selected, the single room schedules that make up the combined room are merged with the combined room schedule to display a single schedule. If a single room that is part of a combined room is selected, the individual room schedule is merged with the combined room schedule. For example, Room A and Room B are configured and can be reserved individually. They are also combined to form Room A + B, which can also be reserved.

If a patron selects Room A + B when making a request, then the room schedule for Room A + B will display the reserved times for Room A, Room B, and Room A + B. The reason for this configuration is that the larger room cannot be reserved if the smaller rooms are already reserved for the same time. If Room A is selected, the schedule for Room A will display the reserved times for Room A and Room A + B. Room A cannot be available if the larger room, Room A + B, is in use at the same time. Prior to the combined room feature, both Room A and Room B would have had to be reserved individually for the same time. That opened the door to a possible reservation problem which in turn made for an unhappy patron, staff member, or both.

CONCLUSION

As libraries serve as community centers and add meeting rooms, auditoriums, and stage areas, a reliable way to administer the use of these spaces is becoming increasingly important. In addition to reliability, the transition of room reservation management to an online system provides increased accessibility. This accessibility is provided through a common interface that is available with nothing more than a web browser as the door to the system, which makes it "portable." The obstacles of finding the keeper of the schedule and making phone or face contact with him during library hours have been removed. Errors will decrease. The dreaded double-booking will be eliminated. The Garden Club, the Youth

Soccer League Board, and the Toastmasters Club will each be able to arrange for their room reservations at their convenience, or the library staff will be able to accomplish this for them, without confusion. The beauty of the database-driven system is that the information displayed on the pages is always fresh and always current. Changes are accommodated immediately, and maintenance is confined to simple data entry regarding new events. There is no clumsy HTML for staff to learn and relearn. The technology solution is the tool to support the service; the service is the provision of the rooms and accompanying equipment for library programs and community groups. The design is successful because the system does not intrude on the task, which is the reservation process. Instead, the process has been streamlined, and access to the process has been expanded.

6 Portals, Gateways, and Directories

There is a general expectation among our patrons that libraries will organize and provide access to valuable resources and services. These are common principles of librarianship. As libraries and information professionals make the "shift" to user-focused services that Jenny Levine writes about, how has the Internet changed the procedures libraries use to implement these principles of organization and access? When Library Information and Technology Association attendees at the American Library Association's 1999 Midwinter Meeting were asked to identify important library technology trends for the future, the top trend identified was "library users who use the Web, expect customization, interactivity, and customer support. Approaches that are library-focused instead of user-focused will be increasingly irrelevant."[1] Gateways and portals are one response to these patron expectations. There is so much "stuff" out there on the Web that quality control can be a significant issue with the use of search engines alone, because there is no human involvement with the selection of the sites that are retrieved by the search engines. Search engines use automated software to assemble details of vast numbers of websites. As collections of databases and local resources, gateways and portals offer a way to provide access to a *recommended* collection of resources, often arranged by subject.

Our websites are a logical door to many of our resources, both local and remote. Many patrons use our websites as starting places for their web browsing, and many parents feel comfortable using us as de facto gateways for their children's web activity, regardless of the actual organization of our websites. Online library catalogs are increasingly functioning as gateways to cataloged web resources as well. At the first plenary session of the Library of Congress's Bicentennial Conference on Bibliographic Control for the New Millennium, Sarah Thomas, university librarian at Cornell University, proposed that library catalogs be adapted to serve as authoritative portals to the Internet. She discussed the traditional library catalog with its forte of reliability and the web portals with their assets of currency and customizability.[2] As libraries have become more technology-savvy, library web gateways are becoming standard access points, or anchor sites. They narrow the search focus of our patrons by offering lists of references, often annotated, that have been reviewed by librarians and subject specialists. Patrons do not want to be restricted to one library catalog for information resources, though. Portals and gateways can offer a way to navigate through many catalogs and databases with a single user interface. They provide more than just a list of sites like those retrieved by a search engine, because the sites that they list have been evaluated. There isn't as much data to wade through when using a gateway, as opposed to using a hit list from a search engine. The user values them because they narrow the path to the target.

PORTALS AND GATEWAYS

Gateways are sometimes called "portals" or "subject directories." Just as often, however, they are given separate though indistinct definitions. The similarity between gateways and directories is that the data listed by both is selected by specialists or librarians. Gateways and directories can both be limited to specific subject areas, such as the Arts and Humanities Gateway of the University of Australia or those of other large universities. The advantage to patrons is that the websites included in subject gateways are generally of a higher quality than those found unselectively by search engines.

The terms "gateway" and "portal" are also often used interchangeably. Michael Looney and Peter Lyman define portals as "systems which gather a variety of useful information resources into a single, 'one stop' Web page, helping the user to avoid being overwhelmed by infoglut, or feeling lost on the Web."[3] Clearly this definition also describes many web *gateways* as well. The home pages of big Internet service providers like America Online (AOL), Yahoo, Microsoft Network, and Excite are commonly called "portals." Their typical content offerings include online shopping, search engines, e-mail, news, stock quotes, weather information, discussion groups, and many other services. Much of this is the type of daily content information that users are routinely interested in, and the advantage of the portal is that the information has been aggregated in a single place. Most of the big portals offer users the opportunity to customize the portal, including changing the page layout and determining the featured content from defined lists of options. So with nothing more than a mouse click the user can see what the weather is in Hometown, USA, as well as what is happening to his stock portfolio in the market today. A twist on this is the "vortal," or vertical portal, which is an industry-specific portal that offers statistics, newsletters, and specialized research data for a particular industry. The Health Sciences Library Portal of the University of Pittsburgh is a good example of specialized content offered to a narrow community.

Many libraries are creating gateway pages on their websites without realizing that is what they are. Many libraries subscribe to online services. These libraries usually have at least a regular HTML-based web page that contains links to online services along with some description of what they are. This is a gateway. It serves as a starting point for patrons to link to other selected resources. A good example of a public library gateway appears on the "eResources" web page of the Clinton-Macomb Public Library (CMPL) website (http://www.cmpl.org/Eresources/Default.asp). Patrons can narrow down the range of links offered by choosing from "Subjects," "Popular Sites," "Topics," and "Magazine and Newspaper Articles." Depending on which one of the four options is selected, the patron is sent in a different direction. Both "Subjects" and "Topics" send the patron to another page on the website that contains a list of links associated with the selected option, along with descriptions for each link. The links under "Popular Sites" send the patrons directly to specific web pages. The "Magazine and Newspaper Articles" button sends the patron to an associated database on a specific website, but first the patron is sent to a page that requires him to enter his library card number before proceeding to the desired site. The eResources page is a single page that directs patrons to preapproved websites. The links to the resulting websites are preapproved because the links are stored in a database that was created and is maintained by a member of the CMPL staff. Figure 6.1 is an example of the CMPL eResources page.

The eResources pages are dynamic in that the items contained in the selection lists are generated from data in a Microsoft Access (MS Access) database. The Clinton-Macomb Public Library wanted to get away from the idea of librarians manually editing HTML code to maintain the website. As websites have grown in complexity, the time-consuming process of coding HTML pages has become a huge task. HTML editors do little to simplify the process; it is still largely manual, and the process must be constantly maintained to ensure that information is current. The more links involved in the process, the clumsier and more impossible the task becomes. Taking a step away from HTML, the Clinton-Macomb system uses a mixture of built-in features of MS Access for the database entry and Active Server Pages (ASPs) for the web interface. MS Access has a built-in form-creation feature that assists in creating data entry forms from tables in the database. Once a form is created, it is used to add and manipulate one record at a time, which simplifies the data entry process. The forms

FIGURE 6.1   EResources page on the Clinton-Macomb Public Library's website

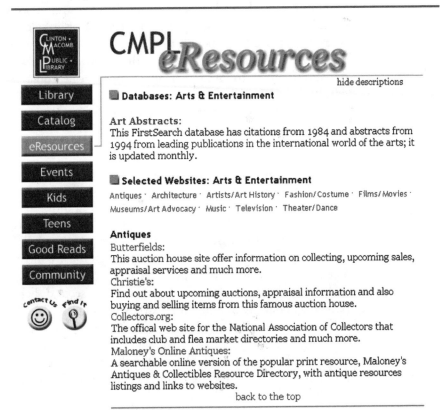

are stored in the database along with the data, so they are not web-based. The person attempting to use the forms and access the database must be at the computer where the database is stored, or have MS Access installed on the local computer and access the database over a network. In either case, the data is entered using the resources provided with the database.

The eResources web pages are generated from the information in the database. The scripting behind the eResources ASP pages queries specific tables in the database to obtain the necessary information to display the selection lists and associated link locations. For the initial eResources page, the "Subjects," "Popular Sites," "Topics," and "Magazine and Newspaper Articles" selection lists are created from information contained in tables in the database. The initial eResources page automatically adjusts as the staff use the MS Access forms to add items to the tables associated with the "Subjects" and other selection lists. In the case of

"Subjects" and "Topics" selections, the specific selection is used to narrow down the actual list of links. The selection is passed to another ASP page that uses the selection to query the database for associated links. The resulting page that is displayed contains a list of link descriptions and link titles, which send the patron to a specific website or web page. The staff members verify each link and enter the information into the tables that tie the specific links to an associated "Subject" or "Topic" list item. Since a database and scripting were used, the web page automatically adjusts as more links are added to the database corresponding to a specific subject or topic.

WHY PORTALS AND GATEWAYS ARE NEEDED

Library staff members control the links stored in the database that make the eResources pages function. This provides two separate benefits. The first benefit is from the staff's perspective. The actual web pages never require updating, because the data in the database controls the web pages. The staff can easily add and correct links in the database, which immediately updates the eResources pages. The second benefit is from the patron's perspective. Since the staff is maintaining the link information, the patron can have a high level of confidence that the displayed list is of links that really go to live pages and are actually associated with the desired subject matter. Additionally, the patron knows that the subjects and links have been reviewed and approved by the library.

CREATING A LIBRARY PORTAL

Library Portal Components

Portals typically offer both a customizable interface to the Web and personalized content. The organization (library or business) customizes the interface, and the customer is permitted some degree of control over personalizing the content or resources on the portal. Library portals organize and offer access to external resources such as full-text articles from premium databases; and offer library-specific services such as patron account information, automatic e-mail notification, and personal event calendars.

A critical component of any library portal is a single-search interface, which provides searching capability across many electronic resources at one time. In order to retrieve various types of resources, the search interface must support various formats, such as MARC and Dublin Core. It must also support various protocols, such as Z39.50 and XML. The most important aspect of this component is convenience. Without a single-search interface, the patron must search library catalogs, capture the information; and search individual databases, again capturing the information. She may have to use different search strategies for each of the searches. The single-search interface offers convenience and simplicity to the user and can access information that the user would not have been able to retrieve with a standard search engine: that of any proprietary databases supported on the portal.

Reference linking is another important portal component. An abstract that is linked to a full-text article is a linked reference; so is a scanned obituary image that is linked to an SQL database entry. Reference linking provides a tremendous time savings to users.

A patron authentication component serves as the door key to restricted parts of the portal. Patron authentication is the process of checking patron information against a database to determine whether the patron is permitted to access resources. Many libraries permit unrestricted access to library, community, and catalog information on their portals, for instance. However, they may require that a user be a card-carrying patron in order to use premium online databases that are also on the portal.

Content enhancement is a portal component that harks back to the Amazon.com ballyhoo. Roy Tennant has said that libraries can do a better job of marketing their print collections by providing better information through book covers, tables of contents, and reviews, among other things.[4] Most standard catalog records do little to enlighten the researcher in this respect. A simple MARC record provides little more than author, title, and subject information about the item in the collection. Users can glean only minimal information about book contents from the record. When a table of contents is integrated into a MARC record, the record becomes an enhanced MARC record. Enhanced MARC records can narrow the focus of any student or casual reader's search. Most of the larger catalog vendors who offer this service have contracted with third-party vendors for its provision, so it doesn't come cheaply. But once again, a business model has driven the library model, and Amazon's practice of providing reviews, book covers, and tables of contents is driving the library market, with several library products supporting content enhancement on the market recently.

A fifth component of portals that is seeing some development is that of interactive services, as noted by Richard Boss.[5] Some portals like Yahoo and AOL support interactive services like chat and e-mail, but library portals typically do not. However, library portals are likely to support customer access to borrowing records, including renewals, holds, and fines. In addition, services like automatic e-mail notification, personal calendars and program registration, online reference, and online summer reading programs are new interactive services that can be supported on library portals.

Personalization versus Customization

The terms "personalization" and "customization" are often used interchangeably, just as the terms "gateway" and "portal" are often substituted for one another. Personalization is frequently discussed within the context of customization, but Jakob Nielsen argues that the terms are different.[6] From his perspective, personalization involves the creation of profile characteristics that are saved somewhere in a database that is a component of the system. The system then serves up information to the user based on a model that it has created from those characteristics. Personalization is thus more complicated than customization. The Mooresville grant project discussed in chapter 3 is an example of a personalized system; Amazon Alerts is another example of a personalized product. Personalization has been also defined as "letting the customer say yes or no to letting a company use personal information, with the opportunity to opt out at any time."[7] Personalization is not a new concept in business. Smart business people have long recognized that the more they know about their customers and what they want, the better prepared they are to provide it.

Customization commonly involves the user making selections from a predefined set of options, such as a list of databases or a list of stocks. Nielsen describes customized pages as being directly controlled by the user. The user can dump all of the stocks on his list and choose new ones. He can elect to look at headlines from the *New York Times* instead of headlines from the *Indianapolis Star,* or be notified of weather conditions at his favorite ski resort instead of those at his alma mater. He has merely made selections from a list of options, which he can change his mind about at any time.

> Personalization is all about providing information that reflects what you know about a customer—and what you know is changing all the time. —Todd Hollowell and Verma Gaurav[8]

The debut of Bank One's Personal Platinum Card was touted recently in television ads. Credit customers may choose from dark green, yellow, or purple cards, each of which is tied to a different billing date and interest rate combination. The purple card, for example, provides a low introductory rate of interest, travel rewards, and an end-of-the-month billing date. Bank One offers potential customers the opportunity to "Choose your rate, your reward, your individual color!" People like choices, and they like to choose services that offer them customized convenience.

Customization of a Gateway

An award-winning example of a "smart" and classy customizable gateway for kids is the brarydog.net site of the Public Library of Charlotte and Mecklenburg (North Carolina) County. Brarydog.net provides patrons the opportunity to customize a homework help web page. Patrons can customize links to their favorite web tools, search engines, and websites. Access to premium web resources and homework help tools is available as part of the brarydog.net product with just a user ID and password. Kids can access their customized reference and homework help site from any computer with Internet access.

The brarydog.net product is convenient, its interface is familiar to the user, and it is customer-focused. It is an example of a tiered portal, because the interface and resources have both been selected for children. The kid is king. He can integrate his favorite resources into his customized electronic collection. A customized gateway such as brarydog.net is also valued for its interface consistency. Upon log-in, the patron sees the same interface each time. He has already customized the settings, so there is no guesswork involved. The customization also provides navigational value. The opportunity for patrons to customize portions of our library websites as personalized web gateways is a logical next step. Patrons can create their own interfaces without having to know any HTML.

> The library's tools, facilities, and infrastructure enable users to create their own information systems: collections consisting of links to information sources relevant for their personal use. —Bas Saveniji and Natalia Grygierczyk[9]

A library gateway such as brarydog.net can also be a valuable tool for marketing the library to a target group, in this case, kids. The gateway is the site of choice, the starting point, and the more things patrons can do on our websites, the more effective our sites will be, both as service points and marketing tools. The library gateway user comes to identify with the library; there is "brand" identification. Corporations market their brands, which they articulate as representative of their product lines, their values and goals, their images, the overall perception of them by the rest of the world. In short, their brands are synonymous with their identities. In the same way, the brarydog.net brand becomes an important part of the Public Library of Charlotte and Mecklenburg County's marketing toolkit.

Customization of a Portal

A well-known example of a personal library portal is MyLibrary. In an effort to reduce information overload, Eric Lease Morgan developed MyLibrary@NCState, a portal-like system based on user profiles. MyLibrary is a customizable interface to library resource collections at North Carolina State University. It is of interest because it is user-centered, using forms to profile user interest, suggesting resources for users, and permitting them to make further selections by adding or deleting from the suggested resource list. It is accessible with a single tool: a web browser.

The system was designed to run on a Unix platform. Perl scripting language was used for generating the web pages and interacting with the database. MySQL was used for the database that housed the information. As Eric Lease Morgan states, "It was chosen primarily because it was free, implements SQL, runs on multiple Unix computers, provides the mechanisms for auto-incrementable fields as well as variable field lengths, but most importantly, it supports an application programmer's interface (API) for both the Perl and C programming languages."[10]

The implementers of MyLibrary reached some of the same conclusions as the automatic e-mail system grant development team at Mooresville. Internal reports run against the MyLibrary databases are a valuable collection development tool, yielding information on which titles, authors, and subjects are selected most frequently by users. MyLibrary developers refer to this by-product of customization as a "double-edged sword," however.[11] This is because the same functionality that gives system administrators the ability to view patron profiles also has the potential of being used against the patron in the event that it is requested by the federal government.

MyLibrary at Cornell University

Other MyLibrary systems have been implemented around the country. MyLibrary at Cornell University Library (http://mylibrary.cornell.edu) is an umbrella service for two other related products, MyLinks and MyUpdates. MyLinks is the tool for personal organization of resources on the MyLibrary page. Patrons can carry their portable bookmarks with them, rather than having to create them on every machine they use, whether it be a home, office, or lab computer. MyUpdates helps researchers stay informed of new resources obtained by the Cornell University Library. The user can choose to be notified of new resources in his area of interest either by e-mail or when logging into his account. Another feature, MyContents, enables users to select subject areas for which they would like to receive the tables of contents of journals in those subjects (a twist on the Amazon Alerts). As described on the website, "MyLibrary is a collection of personal electronic services, developed by the Cornell University Library, that can be customized to reflect your own personal interests and research needs."

Components of the MyLibrary@Cornell Portal   John Fereira, programmer/analyst specialist at Cornell University, offered some insight into the components of the MyLibrary@Cornell project. MyLinks, which was written by Fereira, is essentially a bookmark manager. It allows patrons to capture links found on the web and categorize them into folders. Since the links are managed by a central system, access to the "bookmarks" is available from almost any computer. Another value-added feature in MyLinks that goes beyond using a browser for capturing bookmarks is a form that allows a patron to search the Cornell library's electronic resources collection. This is helpful because the electronic resources collection contains many resources that are not discoverable from a "google" search. Many of these resources are databases or journal aggregators—like Lexis-Nexis, for example—for which Cornell has paid subscription fees.

MyUpdates was introduced shortly after MyLinks. MyUpdates allows patrons to enter their e-mail address and create "search profiles" containing subject matter that they are interested in. The search profiles can be a combination of up to three criteria separated by a Boolean operator: And, Or, or Not. For example, entering "pie And cherry" will result in a search for new items in the collection that contain both the words "pie" and "cherry." The search profile also identifies which library collection or collections to search. A selection list of available library collections is provided from which the patrons choose. Every two weeks the search criterion is checked against new items in the library collection. E-mails are generated from the resulting matches and inform patrons when new items matching their areas of interest have been added to the library collection.

A third service that was introduced in August 2002 is called MyContents. MyContents is a current awareness service that allows patrons to receive the tables of contents of selected journals via e-mail. Cornell receives copies of the tables of contents for almost 1,000 different journals from several vendors. Patrons can browse or search the title list, select the journal or journals of interest, and add them to their Journal Table of Contents list. They can also choose to receive the table of contents in EndNote, ProCite, or Reference Manager file formats. The e-mails are not generated on a timed basis like those of MyUpdates. They are generated when each journal table of contents becomes available.

Hardware and Software   The brawn behind these services stems from an older Sun Ultra 4 dual processor machine with 512 megabytes of memory using Solaris 2.7 as the operating system. Both MyLinks and MyUpdates use Oracle 8.1 for the database. MyContents uses MySQL for storing most of its information, but it also accesses the library management system, which also uses the Oracle database. An Apache web server is used along with Jakarta

About Struts: Java Servlets are designed to handle requests made by web browsers. Java ServerPages are designed to create dynamic web pages that can turn billboard sites into live applications. Struts uses a special Servlet as a switchboard to route requests from web browsers to the appropriate ServerPage. This makes web applications much easier to design, create, and maintain. For further information, see:

http://jakarta.apache.org/struts/faqs/
kickstart.html

http://jakarta.apache.org/tomcat/index.
html

Tomcat. The Jakarta Tomcat handles the Java Servlet and JavaServer pages. Most of the content is generated using Java Servlets. MyContents was written using the Jakarta Struts package, which provides what is called an MVC (Model View Controller).

Almost all of the systems use open-source components, including the JDBC drivers for database access, Jakarta Tomcat and Struts, an open-source database connection pooling API, and the Apache web server. MyContents uses several other technologies, including the Jakarta James mail management system for processing incoming tables of contents and Xalan/Xerces for handling XML (Extensible Markup Language). For MyContents, all incoming tables of contents are converted to XML and then transferred to several formats.

Another project that Fereira is involved in is JA-SIG's uPortal project. "JA-SIG" stands for Java Architectures Special Interest Group. As described on the JA-SIG website (http://www.ja-sig.org/index.html), "uPortal is a free, sharable portal under development by institutions of higher education. This group sees an institutional portal as an abridged and customized version of the institutional Web presence . . . a 'pocket-sized' version of the campus Web."

UPortal is an open-standard effort using Java, XML, JSP, and J2EE. Several JA-SIG member institutions are collaborating on its development. Members can download uPortal and use it on their website at no cost. UPortal is not intended to be an out-of-the-box or "turnkey" portal "solution." Instead, it is a set of Java classes and XML/XSL documents that can be used to produce a portal for use on an institution's website. It will run on any platform that has a Java 2 implementation available for it. According to the FAQ page on the JA-SIG website, JA-SIG members are running uPortal for development and deployment purposes on a number of different platforms, including Microsoft Windows, Solaris, Linux on three different architectures, and MacOS X. The FAQ page also describes the level of expertise necessary to deploy uPortal, and answers a variety of other questions about it.

PURCHASED PORTAL SYSTEMS

There are a handful of major library portal developers who market their systems directly to libraries or to library automation vendors. The opportunities for customization of the purchased interfaces vary widely. In addition, most major automated library system vendors are offering portals as part of their systems, as upgrades or add-ons. There are generally several components supported by these systems, and libraries can select which ones to turn on or turn off. This broadens or narrows a portal's functionality, and it may also affect pricing. While many libraries purchase the portal product marketed by their current automation vendor, it is important to note that there is some flexibility in the marketplace. Some automation vendors will provide stand-alone portal versions of their products to their competitors' customers.

CONCLUSION

Like the interactive services that they increasingly support, the critical and most attractive feature that library portals offer is convenience. Inasmuch as they are customizable, portals also offer relevancy to the individual user. These key service components are likely to remain important as technology marches forward. They level the playing field and keep libraries and their physical collections viable at a time when our customers are flocking to the Internet for information. And libraries are in an ideal position to provide these services better than anyone else, with our pool of organizational talent and our public service mission.

MAJOR PORTAL PRODUCTS[12]

Auto-Graphics Agent
www.auto-graphics.com/ls_agent.html

Dynix Horizon Information Portal
http://www.dynix.com/products/pac/index.asp

Endeavor ENCompass
http://encompass.endinfosys.com/

Ex Libris MetaLib
www.exlibris-usa.com/MetaLib/index.html

Fretwell-Downing ZPORTAL and CPORTAL
www.fdusa.com/products/zportal.html

Gaylord Polaris PowerPAC
www.gis.gaylord.com/

Innovative Interfaces Millennium Access Plus
www.iii.com/html/products/p_map.shtml

The Library Corporation YouSeeMore
www.tlcdelivers.com/tlccarl/products/pacs/
    youseemore.asp

MuseGlobal MuseSearch and Information Connection Engine (ICE)
www.museglobal.com/Products/index.html

Open Knowledge Initiative
http://web.mit.edu/oki/

Sirsi iBistro and iLink
www.sirsi.com/Sirsiproducts/elibrary.html#what

VTLS Chameleon iPortal
www.vtls.com/Products/gateway

WebFeat Knowledge Prism
www.webfeat.org

For detailed information on the products of major library portal developers and library automation vendors, see Richard W. Boss, "How to Plan and Implement a Library Portal," *Library Technology Reports* 38, no. 6 (November/December 2002).

Notes

1. "Technology and Library Users: LITA Experts Identify Trends to Watch," 1999, available at http://www.lita.org/committe/toptech/trendsmw99.htm (accessed 20 December 2002).

2. Sarah E. Thomas, "The Catalog as Portal to the Internet," 21 December 2000, available at http://lcweb.loc.gov/catdir/bibcontrol/thomas_paper.html (accessed 11 January 2003).

3. Michael Looney and Peter Lyman, "Portals in Higher Education," *EDUCAUSE Review* 35, no. 4 (July/August 2000), available at http://www.educause.edu/ir/library/pdf/ERM0042.pdf (accessed 10 February 2003).

4. Roy Tennant, "Digital Libraries—The Convenience Catastrophe," *Library Journal* 126, no. 15 (15 December 2001).

5. Richard W. Boss, "How to Plan and Implement a Library Portal," *Library Technology Reports* 38, no. 6 (November/December 2002).

6. Jakob Nielsen, "Personalization Is Over-Rated," 1998, available at http://www.useit.com/alertbox/981004.html (accessed 10 February 2003).

7. Christopher Chia and June Garcia, "The Personalization Challenge in Public Libraries: Perspectives and Prospects," 2002, available at http://www.bertelsmann-stiftung.de/documents/Personalisation_engl.pdf (accessed 4 February 2003).

8. Todd Hollowell and Verma Gaurav, "Customers Want the Personal Touch," *Information Week* (24 June 2002): 48.

9. Bas Saveniji and Natalia Grygierczyk, "Libraries without Resources: Towards Personal Collections," *Collection Building* 20, no. 1 (2001): 18–24.

10. Eric Lease Morgan and Amy Ising, "My Library: A Manual and Workshop," 2000, available at http://dewey.library.nd.edu/mylibrary/manual/mylibrary-manual.html#id230857 (accessed 3 January 2003).

11. Eric Lease Morgan, "The Challenges of User-Centered, Customizable Interfaces to Library Resources," *Information Technology and Libraries* 19, no. 4 (December 2000).

12. Mary E. Jackson, "The Advent of Portals," *Library Journal* 127, no. 15 (15 September 2002): 36–39.

7 Local History

Online Obituaries, Photographs, and Local Newspaper Articles

For those of us working in libraries, the general pace of technology development seems to be losing little of its apparent acceleration. The explosion of Internet use and the increasing accessibility of that medium have created an expanded sense of community for people everywhere. At the same time, growing numbers of people across the country are narrowing their personal communities through genealogy research. Individuals involved in family history research are a dedicated group, as are the library professionals and local history volunteers who assist them. Local history resources come in many sizes and shapes and are often not in traditional formats. They may include obituaries, marriage records, cemetery records, old photographs, yearbooks, family histories, scrapbooks, and federated club program booklets. Over the years, library staffers and local volunteers in many communities have assembled lists, card files, loose-leaf notebooks, and vertical files filled with records that document the history of their communities, and the residents and events that shaped them.

Access to these treasured records continues to be an issue because they are unique and irreplaceable. While a history grant and dedicated staff can provide for the conservation-quality preservation of a historical photograph collection, this does little to resolve the issue of access. Who gets to use these records and under what conditions? Access to these records is typically restricted to in-house use, and is often under the watchful eye of a local history staff person as well. Even under these controlled circumstances, important documents and photographs have "walked," and photographs have been razored from old yearbooks.

Digitization has afforded a whole new level of access to researchers of genealogy and local history. Core groups of volunteers and staff who once methodically maintained paper files now routinely scan and save digital files for public access. Catalog card file entries of obituary information have made the shift to database entries. Crumbling newsprint obituaries have become scanned image files, and precious yearbook photos have been scanned and linked to student names in a database. Making these updated files available on library websites dramatically increases the public's access to them. Documents that were once perused only occasionally during on-site visits by traveling genealogists are now available to the global community, with nothing more than database tools and a web interface.

ONLINE OBITUARY INDEXES

Many libraries maintain their own obituary indexes for researchers to use. These are made up of index cards and newspaper clippings that take up physical space and can degrade over time. A wealth of genealogical information is contained in these paper indexes and articles. But often this wealth of information is only available to individuals who can visit the library. The information that can be retrieved is also limited by the particular pieces of the genealogical puzzle that a researcher has for the initiation of his search. Wild-card searches and partial searches are not even options in the world of index card files. What about the individual doing research on a family whose descendants are spread across the United States? The researcher usually cannot physically visit every library in every town or county where he believes a family member is buried. If the obituary information is available on the Internet, though, the researcher can make a virtual visit. He can perhaps even create a family tree from the comfort of his home. An online obituary database makes the data available to anyone who is on a computer in the library or has Internet access at home. The records can be searched using keywords, rather than by thumbing through index cards. The space within the library that is typically required for cabinets to house the index cards and shelves to hold the newspaper articles can be reclaimed and used for other purposes.

The Mooresville Public Library had collected some 21,000 obituaries from newspapers and area residents' scrapbook collections over a thirty-year period. The obituaries were loosely organized in notebooks, alphabetically by last name of the deceased, and generally by death date. The three local funeral directors had provided their funeral registries as companion volumes, which include date of death and place of burial. Not infrequently, genealogy researchers have come to the library with only a "piece" of information, perhaps from a remembered conversation with a now-deceased family member. Genealogy patrons have come to the library with some pretty odd and interesting details. They may know the name of a descendant's dog, or the nickname of the brother of the descendant. The items that they can recall from long-ago conversations with a relative may not be the details that are typically included in a paper card file entry. A database is an ideal home for these pieces of data. Imagine being able to search on a long-deceased ancestor's dog's name or the nickname of the descendant and retrieve the record that you need! The obituary notebooks at Mooresville did not lend themselves to points of access beyond the name of the deceased. In addition, many of the older obituaries were crumbling or damaged.

An online obituary system called "Legacy Link" was created for the Mooresville Library that provided for indexing obituary information and scanned images of the obituaries themselves. The library planned to scan each obituary and save the files as image files, which would be linked to entries in a MySQL database. (Information on MySQL is available at http://www.mysql.com/products/index.html.) Each field in the database would be searchable, and the database would be mounted on the library web server. Eventually the library hopes to integrate this information with the vertical files that it maintains on prominent community members, scanning the contents of each file and linking it to the MySQL database. The goal of the project is to organize and provide multiple points of access for the local obituary collection, as well as to provide cross-referencing of the obituaries to other library resources.

Back in 1998, the Plainfield Guilford Township (Indiana) Public Library (http://www.plainfield.lib.in.us) saw the need to convert its index cards into a database. The library chose Microsoft Access, and went so far as to create a web-based front end that allowed patrons to search on first and last names. The library drew responses from across the country within a week of the obituary index going online, and received thanks from many people who could not make the trek to Plainfield to do their research. Over the years, the database grew to the point that the web interface would provide inconsistent results due to time-outs from the number of records that were being searched. The database had grown to the point that transferring it from the master location to the website also caused lockup problems. In response, the Plainfield Library chose to use the system developed for the Mooresville Library.

Components of an Online Obituary System

There are three main components that make up the online obituary system: the *database* that houses the records, the *staff interface* for entering and maintaining records, and the *patron interface* for searching and displaying records. Hard drive space on the web server could be considered a fourth component if scanned images of the obituaries are going to be included. In the Mooresville Library's Legacy Link project, scanned images of the obituaries are linked to the obituary information for download and printing, while the Plainfield Library allows the patron to find the obituary information of interest in an index and send a request for the actual obituary.

Database

The database is the key component that makes an online obituary system function. The web pages are useless without the data in the database. The obituary database is not as complicated as some of the other systems that have been described. It basically consists of one table that contains the fields that make up the obituary, such as "Last Name," "First Name," and "Date of Death." If index cards are currently used for obituary information, the data that is identified on them can help to define the fields that are required for the table in the database. The ultimate goal is to transfer the information from the index cards into the database in a consistent manner so the data can be searched. Breaking down the information on the index cards into specific fields creates the necessary consistency. All of the obituary information will be in the same place and in the same format no matter who enters the information.

Staff Interface

The data transfer between index cards and the database is facilitated by the staff interface. The staff interface is a template that provides an outline for a staff member to enter the data into the database. For the Plainfield Library, the Microsoft Access database was an easy way to get started because Microsoft Access contains built-in functionality for entering, viewing, and manipulating data in the database.

This built-in functionality provided the staff interface for entering the index card information into the database. However, the built-in functionality is only available to those who have Microsoft Access loaded on their computers and have direct access to the database file. If the database file is on a server outside the firewall and cannot be seen over a network, then the built-in functionality is not available and some other method of data entry or updating the database is required. Originally, Plainfield solved this problem by keeping a master version of the database on the library server. The master database would be copied onto the web server every so often. This method worked for years, but as the database grew, so did the problems associated with transferring the database. The file size became so large that the transfer took longer and longer. To add to the problem, people continued to search the database while the newer version was being transferred, which caused lockup problems.

An alternative is the creation of an independent web-based interface for data entry that updates the database that is on the web server. This eliminates the need to copy the database from one place to another, so the data is always fresh. In this scenario, the staff interface consists of a web page for viewing and searching lists of existing entries, a web page for editing existing entries, and a web page for entering new obituaries. The web browser is the only tool, or software, that a staff member needs to keep the database updated. In actuality, the Add and Edit pages are really the same page. When adding, the fields are blank, and when editing, the fields are populated with corresponding information in the database. The fields on the Add and Edit pages correspond to the fields in the database. The staff member fills in the data fields from the index card or actual obituary and submits the information. With an obituary record, there is no guarantee that information for all of the fields will be available. A determination has to be made of what critical pieces of information are required if some form of error checking is desired. For example, a check of the data can be made to ascertain that at least one field contains data and the record is not completely blank. Once submitted and all error checks pass, the data is transferred directly from the page to the database. Figures 7.1 and 7.2 are examples of the staff maintenance pages for listing and adding obituary records.

Patron Interface

The last piece of the online obituary system is the patron interface. Patrons obviously need a way to view the obituaries in the database. A patron is not going to be interested in paging through thousands and thousands of obituary records in order to find the one he is looking for. Therefore, some type of searching capability is a must. This is where databases shine. They are designed to not only house information, but to allow the user to search, sort, and retrieve the data in various ways. The searching and displaying of information is what the patron interface is all about. Plainfield's original system allowed for searching on the first and/or last name on the obituary. This was already a tremendous improvement over digging through index cards to find possible matches. In the newer online obituary system, there are a variety of ways to view obituary records. The patron can click the letter range that matches the first letter of the person's

FIGURE 7.1   Obituary List Maintenance Page

Obituary Maintenance

View and modify existing obituary entries. They can be displayed by clicking the letter range for the first letter of the last name or by clicking on the **Search** button and filling in the desired fields. Records can be sorted by clicking on the column headings. A new obituary can be added by clicking the **New** button.

| Home | [A-C] [D-F] [G-I] [J-L] [M-O] [P-R] [S-U] [V-X] [Y-Z] | Search | New |

LAST	FIRST	MIDDLE	DATE of DEATH	OBIT FILE	OTHER FILE
Abbott	William	B	10/14/1999	View	
Abney	Nettie	B	09/21/1999		
Adams	Thomas	C	09/00/1958		
Aldrich	Mary	E	01/20/1900		
Alexander					View
Allen				05/00/1952	View
Allen				00/00/1970	
Allen	Earle	Allen	10/19/1937		
Allen	Edith		09/28/1914		
Allen	Eliza	M	01/00/1929		

| Prev | | Page 1 of 173 | | Next |

FIGURE 7.2   **Obituary Add Maintenance Page**

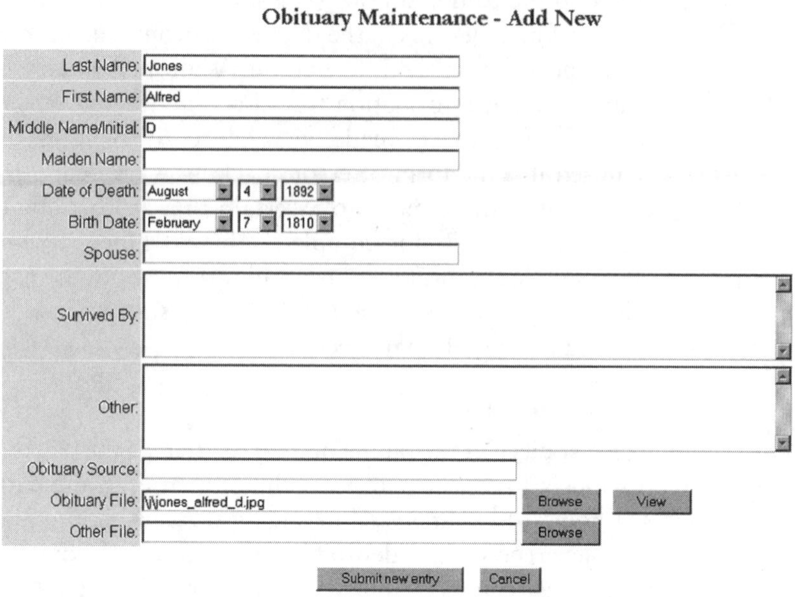

last name. This results in a list of obituary records that are narrowed down to an alphabetical range. The patron can use the search window and fill fields such as "Last Name," "First Name," "Date of Death," "Birth Date," and so on in order to narrow the search. A resulting list is displayed for the matching records; otherwise a message is displayed stating that there were no records found. Each field in the search window represents a field in the database. The more fields that are available for searching, the faster the patron can find what he is looking for. Figure 7.3 is an example of the patron interface with the search window open.

Storing Images

If scanned images of the obituaries are going to be associated with the obituary information, another field must be added and another consideration must be made. There are two options for storing the images. The first option is to store the images directly in the database along with the records. Storing an image in a field in the obituary table along with the associated record makes it easier to display the image once the record is found. However, image file sizes can be very large, which can cause the database to be very large and possibly sluggish.

The second option is to store the image files in folders on the web server's hard drive and store paths to the image file locations in the

FIGURE 7.3   Patron interface with search window open

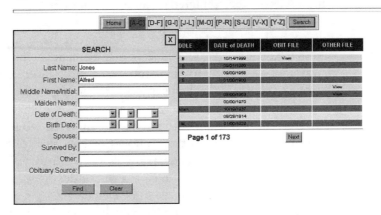

Obituary Finder

Find and view obituaries. They can be displayed by clicking the letter range for the first letter of the last name or by clicking on the **Search** button and filling in the desired fields. Records can be sorted by clicking on the column headings.

database. Storing a path to the file location keeps the database size small. For example, storing a path can vary in size, but the longest path should not be more than 255 characters long. Storing a path name that is 255 characters uses less space than storing the thousands or millions of characters that make up the image file. Depending on how it is handled, the disadvantage of this approach is that if the image file paths change, the path names in the database may need to change. Otherwise, the links are broken. The impact of moving the image files can be minimized by using a relative path to the image file instead of a fixed path. For example, an image file is located on the hard drive at D:\obituaries\images\A\Adams_Fred.jpg. The fixed path is D:\obituaries\images\A\Adams_Fred.jpg. A relative path name assumes that there is a known, default, starting folder path. All path names are based on the path name for the default starting folder. Using the example, the starting folder path is D:\obituaries\images\. The relative path to the image file is A\Adams_Fred.jpg. Only the relative path name is stored in the database, rather than the fixed path name. What if the image is moved to E:\obit\pictures\A\Adams_Fred.jpg? If the fixed path name was stored in the database, the links to the image file would be broken because the location of the image completely changed. All of the path names in the database would have to be updated. If the relative path name was stored in the database, the starting folder path would be changed to E:\obit\pictures\, and all of the links to the image would still work because the stored path stayed the same. However, if the name of Folder A changes to another name like A_Files, the situation is the same as with the fixed path in that the location of the image is completely changed and the links will not work. The important thing to recognize is that the risk of breaking links to the image files is minimized by using the relative path names, as long as those stored relative path names remain the same.

Uses for Other Records

This discussion has centered on an online obituary system. In actuality, the concept can be applied to any information that is indexed. The Plainfield Library had also created Microsoft Access databases for cemetery records and marriage records. The concept and elements behind the online obituary system allowed it to be adapted to handle the cemetery records and marriage records. The fields vary between the obituary, cemetery, and marriage tables, which required changes in the search, add, and edit fields. However, the basic operation stays the same between all three systems. Many libraries have old town photos or historical photos that could be digitized, indexed, and made available on the Internet by using the same concept as the online obituary system. Indexing yearbooks is another application that would use the same elements.

The same rationale that gave credence to moving from paper card catalogs to OPACs also justifies moving paper obituary indexes and other indexed information to searchable online databases. With old card catalogs, how long did it take for someone to find a book when he knew only part of a title? That is assuming he could find it at all. Today with the online catalog, how long does it take someone to find a book using a partial title? Is it minutes or seconds? Apply that same issue to genealogy research. With only a partial piece of information available to approach the search process, a database search might actually be the only way to find the information.

HISTORICAL PHOTOGRAPHS AND DOCUMENTS

The Baltimore County Public Library offers a unique historical photograph service on its website. Updated daily, the Baltimore County Legacy Web (http://www.bcpl.info/lw/index.html) provides a searchable archive of over 11,000 digitized photographs of Baltimore city and Baltimore County. The entries are annotated to include date, photographer, and source information. Entries are indexed alphabetically by topic, and include scanned images and photographs. The researcher may also order prints of many of these photographs in a variety of sizes and photographic treatments. A link takes the viewer to a web page that provides ordering information.

LOCAL NEWSPAPER ARTICLE INDEX

The Missoula (Montana) Public Library has been indexing the local daily newspaper, the *Missoulian,* since the mid-1970s. The index is heavily used by people both in and outside of Missoula County. The library fields requests for copies of information from all over the country. When the *Missoulian* receives an inquiry about its archives, the newspaper always directs the caller to the library. The index began as a card file. When the Missoula Public Library automated in 1991, the records were added to the Dynix system over time, in addition to indexing of the current daily issues of the *Missoulian*. The process was fairly simple, though time-consuming. The staff used the Dynix Community Resources module to list articles by title, author, and subject, as well as by section, page, and column. Each entry became a new record in the database.

In the past couple of years, the *Missoulian* has established a website with an "Archives" link. The library followed this closely, to determine whether it was complete and robust enough to replace the library's in-house index residing on the Dynix system. The *Missoulian* website provides full text and some back-issue browsing, but the *Missoulian* archives product has not shown enough promise to warrant a migration, so the library has continued its indexing project in-house.

The process of local newspaper indexing at the Missoula Public Library goes something like this. One of the reference librarians cruises through the *Missoulian,* marking articles to index. The criteria for selection are that the article has local or state significance. National stories are not considered. The reference librarian often identifies a subject heading, using an authority index created by reference staff. Library volunteers then go through the newspapers and enter all of the marked entries into the database.

In late 2002 the Missoula Library migrated to Sirsi, which signaled changes for the index. Because the Missoula Public Library is part of a seventeen-library consortium for the Sirsi catalog project, the number of individual bibliographic records it holds has special significance for the library; the service cost is determined by the total number of bib records. The Dynix newspaper index hosts over 180,000 records, so the library knew it must develop a separate web-based platform for it.

Fortunately, a department of the Montana State Library, the Montana Library Network (http://montanalibraries.org), hosts a Montana magazines index. The Missoula Library was able to migrate its homegrown database records there. The Montana Library Network staff has created a template for data entry that is Microsoft Access-based, and the volunteers now use the template to enter data in a real-time environment. The new template functions pretty much like the original template for data entry; there are fields for entry of an abstract and up to three subject headings. There are also fields for author, title, date, and section, page, and column. The Missoula Public Library plans to digitize its numerous obituary files and cemetery indexes and mount those on the Missoula Library Network site in the future.

8 Online Summer Reading Registration, Tracking, and Statistics

Summer reading programs make libraries shine. They are our commendable attempt to attract kids to our libraries and keep them reading throughout the summer months. Librarians and teachers know that summer reading programs have positive long-term effects on the reading levels of kids who participate.[1] Many libraries wholeheartedly promote summer reading, pulling out all the stops and adding new bells and whistles to their programs each year. Well-funded summer reading programs can reach epic proportions, with exciting program opportunities and inspired program themes. Those that are not well-funded through the Friends of the Library or the operating budget require additional effort to fund; they may attract innovative funding through some other venue, either grants or underwriting by local businesses. Stories, plays, puppet shows, concerts, games, treasure maps, and magic shows are all pieces of the summer reading structure. It all comes together through a tremendous amount of effort and organization on the part of youth services departments, and it is well worth it.

WHY AN ONLINE SUMMER READING SYSTEM IS NEEDED

The well-planned hype and build-up to summer reading programs have succeeded in attracting increasing numbers of juvenile readers. Kids respond to school visits by youth services librarians, as well as to the advertising for many wonderfully conceived and highly creative programs. And yes, they also sign up to be eligible for the prizes and awards that come with finishing the programs. In addition, many adults are expressing an interest in participating in adult summer reading programs. In fact, this type of programming spans readers in the primary, preschool, intermediate, young adult, adult, and family groups. There are so many components to a summer reading program, and so many library staffers are involved, and so many participants registered, that the potential for miscues and miscommunication is very high. You can almost see the circulation staff rolling their eyes as the program is explained to them at a staff meeting.

"Let's see, who gets the red folders again? How many times can a child get a prize? Does she get a 10-point prize or two 5-point prizes? *You want us to do what with the book reports?!*" The youth services staff is attempting to track the kids' progress through the program, track their attendance at program activities, and keep track of who finishes and whether they got their prizes. They are valiantly trying to attract increasing numbers of kids to register for the programs and to participate in the related programming activities. If summer reading was a PowerPoint presentation, the three main bullets would be registration, tracking, and program completion. Libraries want and need statistics for all three of these components. But beyond needing the statistics, they need a manageable way to obtain them. Once they have the statistics, they can make better decisions about purchasing incentives and awards for the program, which is an important piece of the funding picture. Many summer reading programs could be run on a shoestring but for the cost of the incentives. Great record-keeping would contribute to having great data on which to base decisions for award purchases. So what exactly are the obstacles to getting the statistics that we need?

Summer Reading Program Registration

If the program registration is not simple and straightforward enough, staff may not be able to provide accurate program information to kids and their parents at sign-up. The program director may not be available when each child comes in to register, and youth services staff may be involved with other patrons, so the circulation desk often becomes a default point of contact for summer reading participants. This is especially an issue in small and medium-size libraries. The first week of summer reading registration is a special kind of madhouse. It's hard to make it simple. It's difficult to streamline it. And in an effort to make it fresh and new and attractive to an ever-larger group of participants, we keep changing and refining the way that we organize the overall program. We rely on staff to give correct information every time, to every participant, so we rely on staff to understand it first. When we give that job to front-line staff who already have many things to remember and many situations to deal with, the temporary overload typically doesn't motivate them to pay close attention to the task.

Additionally, the registration process involves collecting data on our program participants that we may have collected before, but that data collection was someplace else, for some other program. Or we already have it but it is in pieces. For instance, we may have names and addresses in the patron database and ages on the Story Time sign-up lists. We need the data again so we go through the process of recording it once more. It is time consuming, and it very likely requires additional staff, if the library has the luxury of scheduling them. If that luxury is not an option, other services can quite literally grind to a halt as the available staff handles an influx of up to hundreds of program registrants who want to get started immediately. The registration window is typically pretty small, and program sign-up puts a squeeze on everyone involved.

Summer Reading Program Tracking

The sheer volume of participants in a successful summer reading program is the balance-tipper in this whole scenario. It's one thing to track twenty kids' progress, and another thing altogether to track the progress of several hundred kids. In any case, it is a challenge to track it *at all*, given all the different components that most programs have. As libraries try to draw increasing numbers into summer reading programs, they are also expanding the scope of the programs to include more age groups. This requires configuring the architecture of summer reading programs in such a way as to provide reading opportunities to several different reading or age levels.

If tracking the program participation is complicated, it is unlikely to be accurately tracked by anyone outside the youth services department, and reasonably so. Both child and parent can be disappointed when they find out they are ineligible for a prize or program because of an incomplete mission log. Obviously, kindergartners will have different program requirements than middle-school age children, and adult readers will have different requirements altogether. The various age groups add complexity to the program, and this adds to the frustration of staff members outside the youth services department who may catch the overflow. In some cases, the outside staff may just give up on it because it has become so complex. The same kids may get rewarded twice for the same benchmarks because they have talked to two different people, one in the children's department and one in circulation. By the time the circulation staff gets the tracking drill down to a fine art, the summer reading program is over and kids are shopping for school clothes.

Summer Reading Program Completion and Awards

If final program instructions are not easy enough to be interpreted by circulation and other staff members, kids who finish the program will only be able to log their completion and receive their rewards when certain staff members are available. This can result in parents having to make more than one trip to register their kids as having completed the program. Of course, this is frustrating to the child who is there to get the long-awaited reward, and it is frustrating to the parent who has to make a second trip to accomplish this.

The incentives or rewards themselves are a whole different type of problem. Just how many prizes should you buy? You can make a guess at how many kids will sign up based on statistics of past years, as well as approximately how many kids will finish the program and be eligible for the prizes. But what if the program has several levels and the child is eligible for a prize at the completion of each level? Maybe each child could actually get a total of ten prizes if he or she finished the entire reading program and completed all of the necessary requirements. Your mission, whether you want to accept it or not, is to try to determine what percentage of program participants will get to receive the entire possible number of prizes. What percentage of them will only get halfway through? You have to provide prizes for every level of program finisher. Here is where you get to bring out your crystal ball, because you don't want to be left with extra stuff. The extra stuff can be reused, but that isn't optimal, since libraries do so much theme-related programming. It would be nice to have a reliable way of tracking kids' progress through the different program levels in order to be able to pull out some dependable statistics that would help you here. It would be great to be able to sort and combine and extract and, well . . . use a database. But how would you use the database, exactly? Who would use it, and where?

TRACKING SUMMER READING ONLINE

The whole summer reading process is a double-edged sword. As the program's popularity grows and the community grows, the process of handling the registration grows. The more effectively a library markets its summer reading program, the bigger the job for the library staff to support it. The elements that make up a summer reading program require very manual tasks that staff members contend with year after year. The manual tasks become clearer by breaking down the elements of the summer reading program. That is to say, they become clearer to the people who do not have to handle summer reading programs. They are probably quite clear to those who already live with these programs.

Many libraries use paper registration sheets that the participant or guardian of the participant fills out and turns in, or the library staff takes down the information and fills out the registration sheet. Depending on how the registration is handled, participants who are in more than one reading program may have to repeat the standard registration process multiple times. Once a participant is registered, another paper sheet is generally used for tracking or logging his or her progress. This sheet is typically filled out by either the patron or a staff member. How are prizes or milestones determined? Someone has to tally the paper progress sheets, which can lead to another internal progress sheet to track each program's progress. Once the summer reading programs end, and the staff stops celebrating, the numbers game begins. All of the information is gathered sheet by sheet, tallied, and turned into percentages and statistics. A summary of the administrative elements of a typical summer reading program includes registration, logging, and reporting. All of these elements can be made less manual and more automated by creating a summer reading system that uses electronic forms that interact with a database.

Online Registration

The registration process is best examined as two pieces. The first piece deals with the gathering of patron information during registration. The second piece involves the actual program registration, or enrollment. The patron information—name, address, age, grade, and so on—must be captured before the patron can actually enroll in a program. By breaking this data into separate pieces, the patron registration information only needs to be captured one time and can then be used for multiple program enrollments.

Patron Registration

The paper registration form can be converted into an online Patron Registration Page, or form. This form consists of name and address information as well as age and grade. The advantage to the online form is that drop-down menus can be utilized and default entries for area code, zip code, city, state, etc., can be used. The drop-down menus and default information speed up the registration process. Once the form is submitted, the patron information is stored in a database, or because of additional checking, a message will be displayed showing that there was a problem with the data entry. A correction can then be made immediately instead of catching it later and trying to correct it after the fact. The possibilities then expand. Patrons can register themselves and staff members can have an easier and more controlled method for registering them. Figure 8.1 is an example of a Patron Registration Page.

Program Registration

However, that only covers the first piece of the overall registration process. The enrollment piece of the registration process is a matter of associating a registrant with a program. The first step is to create a list of available programs and their associated criteria. The list is stored in a table in the database along with the criteria. For example, there may be a program

FIGURE 8.1   Patron Registration Page

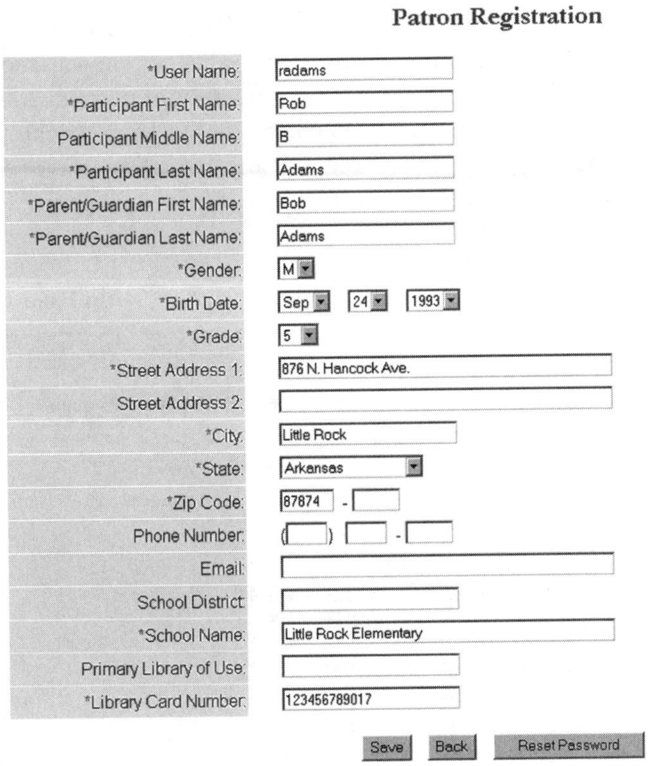

Patron Registration

*User Name:	radams
*Participant First Name:	Rob
Participant Middle Name:	B
*Participant Last Name:	Adams
*Parent/Guardian First Name:	Bob
*Parent/Guardian Last Name:	Adams
*Gender:	M ▾
*Birth Date:	Sep ▾ 24 ▾ 1993 ▾
*Grade:	5 ▾
*Street Address 1:	876 N. Hancock Ave.
Street Address 2:	
*City:	Little Rock
*State:	Arkansas ▾
*Zip Code:	87874 -
Phone Number:	( ) -
Email:	
School District:	
*School Name:	Little Rock Elementary
Primary Library of Use:	
*Library Card Number:	123456789017

[Save] [Back] [Reset Password]

named "Kids Read" for ages seven to ten, or it could be for grades one to four. The idea is to allow only those registrants who meet the specified criteria to enroll in the program. Because the saved registrant information contains age and grade information and the program list contains age and grade restrictions, the system can be programmed to only allow registrants to enroll in a given program who meet the criteria for that program. This can be taken a step further, and the system can be programmed to display a list of available registrants. The staff can choose from the list of registrants who qualify to enroll in the program. This can greatly reduce errors of enrolling registrants in the wrong programs and can speed up the enrollment process.

The system can also be programmed to automatically control the enrollment. Each program is going to have a starting and ending enrollment date, as well as a maximum number of participants. Starting and ending enrollment dates and the maximum number of participants can be saved along with the program criteria in the table. The staff could configure the program settings well in advance. The system would use the starting and ending enrollment dates to verify that a specific program is open for enrollment before allowing anyone to attempt to enroll in the program. After enrollment starts, the system can continuously check the enrollment level by using the maximum number of participants. Once the maximum number of participants has been reached, the system can automatically close the program and not allow anyone else to enroll. Figure 8.2 is an example of a Summer Reading Program Setup Page.

FIGURE 8.2   Summer Reading Program Setup Page

'Summer Readers' Program

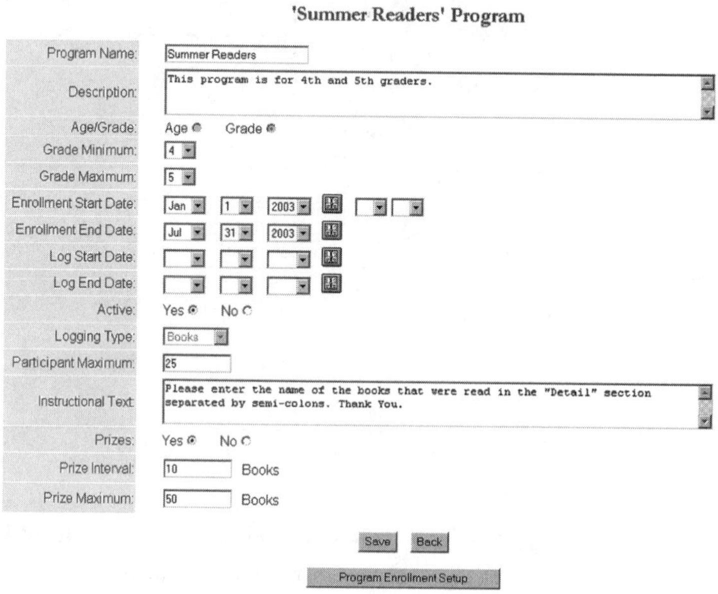

Components of an Online Registration System

From a technical standpoint, the registration process requires three tables within the database. The first table is used to store the patron registration information and associated identification numbers. The fields in the table are associated with the fields on the Patron Registration Page. Some of the fields in the table include "First Name," "Last Name," "Age," "Grade," "Address," "City," "State," "Zip," and "Identification Number." The identification number can be automatically generated by the database. It is used to associate the patron information with a unique number. As each

Patron Registration form is submitted, the data from the form is stored in the table. The information becomes a new record in the Patron Information table with an associated unique identification number.

The second table is used to house the program information, such as the program name and requirements. Some of the fields in the program table include "Program Name," "Description," "Requirement Type," "Minimum," "Maximum," "Start Date," "End Date," "Participant Maximum," and "Identification Number." The "Requirement Type" field would contain a value or string that represents whether age or grade is required for a specific program. The "Minimum" and "Maximum" fields would contain values for the minimum and maximum ages or grades that are allowed for the program, depending on what was entered in the "Requirement Type" field. The "Start Date," "End Date," and "Participant Maximum" fields would be used for automatic enrollment control. As in the Patron Information table, the identification number would be used to associate a unique number with each summer reading program. Generally there is more than one summer reading program. This method allows for as many summer reading programs as the library can handle. As each program is configured using the Summer Reading Program Setup Page and submitted, it is saved as a separate record in the Program Information table and given a unique identifier.

The third table is used to associate patrons with reading programs. The system has to first determine that a patron is eligible for a reading program by comparing the age or grade information stored in the Patron Information table to the minimum and maximum ages or grades stored in the Program Information table. If the patron's age or grade is within range, then the patron can enroll in the program, which is a matter of associating the patron identification number with the reading program identification number. This is where the unique identification numbers come into play. The Enrollment table only needs to contain two fields, "Patron Identifier" and "Program Identifier." The "Patron Identifier" field contains the unique identification number associated with a specific patron. The "Program Identifier" field contains the unique identification number associated with a specific reading program. Each record becomes an association between a patron identification number and a program identification number. For a single program, there will be multiple records in the Enrollment table that contain unique patron identification numbers and the same program identification number. For example, a reading program is stored in the Program Information table and has an identification number of 100. There are two records in the Patron Information table that are within the age or grade requirements for the program. The two patron records have identification numbers of 11 and 33. After the patrons are enrolled in the reading program, the Enrollment table shown in figure 8.3 would contain the following:

FIGURE 8.3 Sample Enrollment table

Patron ID	Program ID
11	100
33	100

The patron and program information are associated because the unique identifiers are associated. Using SQL statements, enrollment lists can be generated by searching for all patron identifiers and program identifiers where the program identifier is equal to a specific program identification number. This will return a list of all the patrons who have registered for a specific program. Figure 8.4 is an example of a summer reading Enrollment List.

Online Logging and Tracking

The registration process is only the beginning of a summer reading program. The ongoing processes of logging and tracking continue throughout the program. The tracking and logging of the participants' reading progress varies from library to library. Individual progress is logged in a

FIGURE 8.4 Enrollment List

'Summer Readers' Program Enrollment

View or Modify existing registration entries by double-clicking on the row. Add a new registration by clicking the Add New Patron button or add an existing registration by clicking the Add Registered Patron button. Delete registration entries by clicking the check boxes and clicking the Delete button.

DELETE	Last Name	First Name	Birth Date	User Name
☐	Adams	Rob	9/24/1993	radams
☐	Adley	Patricia	6/14/1993	padley
☐	Austin	Denise	9/1/1995	daustin
☐	Crew	Nancy	2/20/1994	ncrew
☐	Franks	Cecilia	6/18/1994	cfranks
☐	Haldon	Jake	12/23/1993	jhaldon
☐	Hopper	Opal	6/3/1994	ohopper
☐	James	Tom	6/21/1993	tjames
☐	Jones	Nick	1/7/1994	njones
☐	Osgood	Kira	9/3/1995	kosgood

Prev   Records 1 - 10 of 13   Next

Add New Patron   Add Registered Patron   Delete   Search

Back

variety of ways, such as number of hours, minutes, pages, books, and so on. Prize levels and increments also vary from library to library. Some libraries give a prize for every so many hours, minutes, pages, or books read, while others give prizes at the end of the program no matter how much reading was accomplished. The individuals responsible for logging also vary between libraries. Some libraries have patrons keep their own logs, while others require patrons to report their progress to the staff who then log the progress. In all of these cases, the summer reading system can be expanded to handle the logging and tracking process.

By setting the type of logging, the prize intervals, and the maximum level of prizes, the summer reading system can be programmed to handle the logging and tracking of participants' progress. As was shown in figure 8.2, extra fields such as "Logging Type," "Prize Interval," and "Prize Maximum" are added to the Summer Reading Program Setup Page. In turn, the same fields are also added to the Program Information table. This provides each program with its own method of logging progress, along with its own levels of progress. So, for example, the reading programs for children can be structured to offer prizes more often than the teen reading programs. The system uses this information to know when a participant is eligible for a prize. However, the system cannot know when participants are eligible for prizes unless the logging record is also available. Figure 8.5 is an example of a Log Information Page.

FIGURE 8.5   Log Information Page

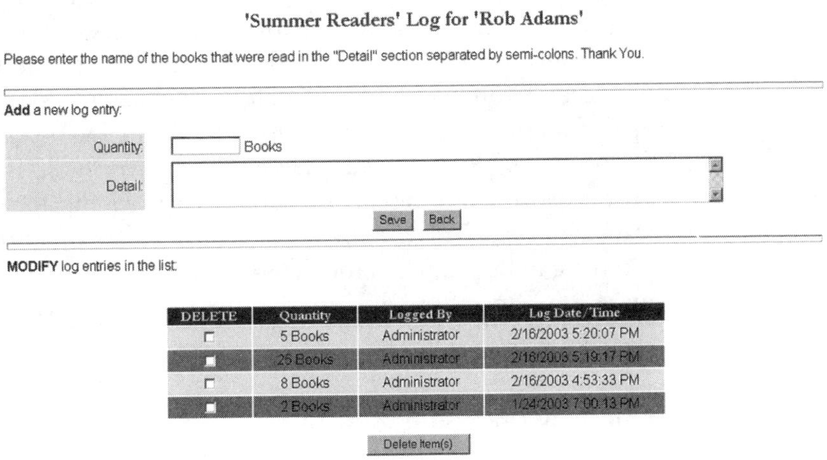

'Summer Readers' Log for 'Rob Adams'

Please enter the name of the books that were read in the "Detail" section separated by semi-colons. Thank You.

Add a new log entry:

Quantity: _____ Books

Detail: _____

Save   Back

MODIFY log entries in the list:

DELETE	Quantity	Logged By	Log Date/Time
□	5 Books	Administrator	2/16/2003 5:20:07 PM
■	25 Books	Administrator	2/16/2003 5:19:17 PM
□	8 Books	Administrator	2/16/2003 4:53:33 PM
■	2 Books	Administrator	1/24/2003 7:00:13 PM

Delete Item(s)

Log Information Page

The Log Information Page shown in the figure is divided into two sections, Add and Modify. The Add section allows for a quantity of books to be entered, along with the details of what was read. Once the "Save" button is clicked, the information is saved into a Log table in the database. The Log table is similar to the previously discussed registration tables. It contains such fields as "Unique Identification Number," "Program Identifier," "Patron Identifier," "Quantity," "Details," "Time Stamp," and "Logged By." The program and patron identifiers are the same unique identification numbers that were described in the registration section. The quantity and details come from the data entered in the Add section of the Log Information Page. The database automatically generates the time stamp in order to record when the entry was logged. Since the Log Information Page is web-based, the participant can log his or her own progress, if so desired. The "Logged By" field would be used for keeping track of who logged each item, staff or patron.

The second section of the Log Information Page is for viewing and modifying the log information. All of the log entries are displayed so that staff or patrons can modify their own information logs. The information is pulled from the Log table that has a matching program identification number and patron identification number in the "Program Identifier" and "Patron Identifier" fields. A resulting match means that there is at least one log entry. All of the associated log entry fields ("Quantity," "Logged By," and "Time Stamp") are displayed. A similar View Only Page can be created that only displays the log information and does not allow any modifications.

Once the quantities are captured, the system has all of the information necessary to track the status of all registrants. The system can compare the program identifier and quantity totals for a given patron identifier in the Log table to the program identification number and prize levels in the Program Information table to determine whether the patron associated with the patron identifier is eligible for a prize. An Alerts Page can be created from this information to show the staff which registrants are eligible for prizes. A "Prize Issued" flag can be added for staff members to clear once a patron receives his or her prize, providing for central control of tracking prizes. This greatly reduces the chances of a program participant receiving multiple prizes for the same level of completion because two or more staff members did not realize that the participant had already received his prize.

Online Reports and Statistics

For most libraries, summer reading doesn't end when the programs are over. It becomes time to tally the results and generate the statistics; it's reporting time. This generally means a manual process of reviewing mounds and mounds of paper to gather the necessary data in what can be a labor-intensive, time-consuming process. With hundreds of registrants and multiple programs, there are bound to be inaccuracies in the tallied results. All of this can be eliminated with the last piece of the summer reading system.

Since the paper logs were converted to online logs and the data is stored in the database, the reporting process is greatly simplified. A combination of scripting and SQL commands can reduce the hours, and in some cases days, of dredging through paper to minutes or seconds. The system can be programmed to manipulate the data stored in the tables and display the results in a web page. Resulting counts, percentages, and other statistical information can be displayed and printed with the click of the mouse. If a database is used that supports Open Database Connectivity or has an export function, then the data can be imported into Excel, Crystal Reports, or other programs that have reporting tools and graphing capabilities.

The key to the overall system is storing the necessary data in the database. If the data is stored in a logical format, the scripting, web pages, and SQL commands can be used to add and modify the data in the database. The benefit for the staff is a considerable reduction in the number of paper forms that have to be handled and a reduction in the time spent collating the results of the summer reading program. The ultimate goal of this feature is to gather the information as quickly and accurately as possible after the programs are complete and generate the reports. Once the reports are over, so are the summer reading programs, and everyone can start looking forward to the fall reading programs to begin!

Note

1. Walter Minkel, "Study: Summer Reading Helps Students," *School Library Journal* 48, no. 2 (February 2002): 24.

9 Providing Online Access to Users without a Library Card

Libraries now have the option of providing patrons with services beyond the walls of the library buildings. With the advent of online subscription services such as Facts on File News Service, Learning Express's Learnatest.com, and other online databases, libraries can add links to their websites to direct patrons to their premium subscription services. Most of these services require that a library card number or personal identification number (PIN) be entered in order to use the service. (There may be contractual obligations with the online subscription vendor that require tighter control, such as that described in the next chapter's discussion of proxy servers.) In this way, a library patron is "authenticated" as being part of the community authorized to access the protected services. This works well for those patrons who actually have a card in hand. However, there are some libraries that would like to provide the opportunity for *potential* library patrons to have access to the services. There are also libraries that are interested in providing the option for people anywhere to use the services, even those individuals outside the library service district. These libraries need a way to give the patrons a number that will authenticate them for the purpose of using the online services. What are their options?

ONLINE TEMPORARY LIBRARY CARDS

The easiest and most straightforward option is to post a temporary library card number on the library website. The card number would allow potential patrons and people from around the world to access the online services. With this method, however, the library would not have a way to track these users. A more effective method is to use a temporary library card issuing system. The system requires people who desire access to the online services to fill out an online form for a temporary library card number. The information is then stored in a database for the staff to review.

In addition to temporary library card management, this type of system provides two more services. Since the person who would like to use the online service must fill out a form, this can act as a deterrent to those who are not legitimately interested in the service or who might abuse the privilege with the temporary card number. The system also functions as a stepping-stone for patrons interested in obtaining a permanent library card. It provides a quick way for the staff to create a permanent library card for the patron who has already been issued a temporary card number, since the data from the online form is already stored in the database. A staff member can pull up the information and cut and paste it into the automated system used to create permanent patron records. Since the information was entered by the patron via the online form, the staff member does not have to retype the information while the patron waits. Some libraries have contemplated automatically issuing a permanent library card from temporary card requests. Others have experimented with cutting and pasting the information into the automation system, just short of issuing the actual card, in order to reduce the patron's wait time when he arrives at the library.

COMPONENTS OF AN ONLINE TEMPORARY LIBRARY CARD SYSTEM

To review an example from the patron's perspective, the system procedure establishes that a patron fill out an Online Request Page and submit the information. If the information is entered correctly, the system issues the patron a temporary library card number while it simultaneously captures the data from the form. If the patron uses the same first name, last name, and phone number to ask for another temporary card, the system notifies the patron that he has already been issued a card. The example system is also designed to rotate temporary library card numbers from a specified list, so that one card number is used for a week and then another is rotated in the next week, and so on.

From the staff's perspective, there is a maintenance page that contains links to a Current Requests Page, Purge Old Requests Page, and Card Number Entry Page. These maintenance pages allow the staff to view and delete current requests, purge requests from the history file, and add card numbers to the card number list. All of this is built around a database.

Patron Interface

We'll begin with the patron interface. The Online Request Page requests the same essential information that is required to issue a permanent library card. There is also an option available to add some additional questions or to require additional information. The standard entry items are "Last Name," "First Name," "Middle Name or Initial," "Street Address," "City," "State," "Zip," "Home Phone Number," "Date of Birth," and "E-Mail." Other items can be added, such as questions about student status or confirmation that the policy is understood. All of the fields on the entry form translate into fields in a Card Request table. Figure 9.1 is an example of the Online Request Page.

After the patron submits this information, the system checks the required fields to be certain that all data is correct. The system also checks to be sure that the individual making the request has not already received a temporary card number. If he has not, the data is saved in the Card Request table.

After the data is saved, the system gets the next temporary library card number from the Card List table and displays it for the patron to use. Anyone in the world can access the online form and submit a request for

FIGURE 9.1   Online Request Page

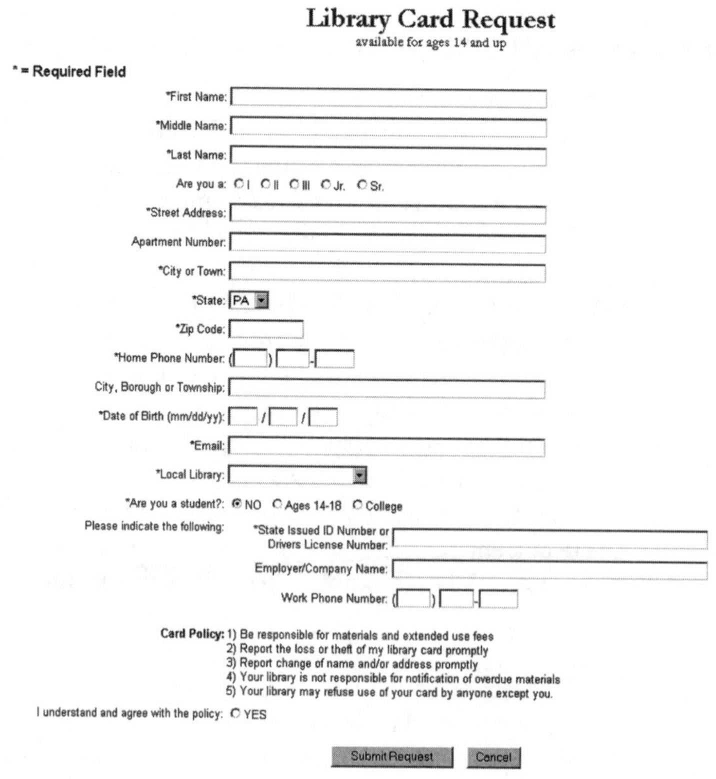

Library Card Request
available for ages 14 and up

* = Required Field

*First Name:
*Middle Name:
*Last Name:
Are you a: ○ I ○ II ○ III ○ Jr. ○ Sr.
*Street Address:
Apartment Number:
*City or Town:
*State: PA
*Zip Code:
*Home Phone Number: (   )   -
City, Borough or Township:
*Date of Birth (mm/dd/yy):   /   /
*Email:
*Local Library:
*Are you a student?: ● NO ○ Ages 14-18 ○ College
Please indicate the following: *State Issued ID Number or Drivers License Number:
Employer/Company Name:
Work Phone Number: (   )   -

Card Policy: 1) Be responsible for materials and extended use fees
2) Report the loss or theft of my library card promptly
3) Report change of name and/or address promptly
4) Your library is not responsible for notification of overdue materials
5) Your library may refuse use of your card by anyone except you.

I understand and agree with the policy: ○ YES

Submit Request   Cancel

a temporary library card. Some libraries want to offer that as an option. For those libraries that would like to let anyone from anywhere request a temporary card number, the form would be left open for just about any entry in all of the fields. The "State" field would have a drop-down selection list for all states, and the "Zip" field would have a text box for entering the zip code. However, for those libraries that only want local patrons to request a temporary card, some of the fields would be more controlled and not left open. For example, the "State" field could be a fixed field that cannot be changed and the "Zip" field could be fixed or a drop-down selection list of available zip codes that pertain to the library's service district. These restricted fields cannot prevent someone outside of the library's area from requesting a temporary card number, but they make it quite clear that the card is only designed for those who live in the area.

Staff Maintenance Pages

The staff can view the patron requests that are saved in the database by using the Current Requests Maintenance Page. This page pulls out all of the requests that are stored in the Card Request table and displays them in a list. Along with the list, there are options that allow the staff to delete and view individual requests. The staff can view an individual record, which also allows them to cut and paste the information into the automated system that is used for permanent library cards. When the staff deletes a request, the request is not permanently deleted. It is removed from the Card Request table and saved to the Card Request History table. This table is a mirror image of the Card Request table. Figure 9.2 is an example of the list of card requests, and figure 9.3 is an example of an individual request from the Card Requests Maintenance Page.

FIGURE 9.2   Card Request list

Card Request Maintenance

CARD REQUESTS

DELETE		REQUESTED ON	NAME	PHONE	STUDENT STATUS	CARD NUMBER
☐	VIEW	12/12/2002	Frank D Post	(111) 111-1111	NO	123456789
☐	VIEW	2/18/2003	Todd D Cutler	(317) 446-6979	NO	987654321
☐	VIEW	2/18/2003	Rob S Cullin	(317) 509-3286	NO	987654321
☐	VIEW	2/18/2003	Doug P Keaton	(317) 555-5555	NO	987654321

Delete

Back to Maintenance Page

FIGURE 9.3   Individual card request

Card Request Maintenance

Card Number: 987654321

Last Name: Cutler

First Name: Todd

Middle Name: D

Suffix:

Street Address: 1455 Renee Dr

Apartment Number:

City or Town: Plainfield

State: IN

Zip Code: 46168

Home Phone Number: (317) 446-6979

City, Borough or Township:

Date of Birth (mm/dd/yy): 03/30/68

Email: toddc@e-vancedsolutions.com

Library: Martin

Student Status: NO

State Issued ID Number or Drivers License Number: 12345

Employer/Company Name: E*vanced Solutions

Work Phone Number: (317) 446-6979

[Cancel]   [Delete]

The Card Request History table contains a history of all card requests that the system uses to determine if someone has already requested a card. If a person's first name, last name, and home phone number appear in the Card Request table or Card Request History table, then he has already been issued a card. The system will notify him that he already has a temporary card number instead of issuing him another. The staff maintains the Card Request History table by using the Purge Old Requests Maintenance Page. This page lists all of the requests that are stored in the Card Request History table. The old requests can be viewed, allowing the data to be cut and pasted into other applications. The page also allows the staff to purge old records by selecting a date. All of the records in the Card Request History table that are older than the selected date are permanently deleted from the table. This also means that any person requesting a temporary library card number who was previously issued a temporary card number, but whose record was removed from the history table, will receive a new temporary library card number. Figure 9.4 is an example of the Purge Old Requests Maintenance Page.

FIGURE 9.4   Purge Old Requests Maintenance Page

Card Request History

The Card Request History Table contains all of the card requests. It should be purged occasionally to remove old requests.

Click on the calendar icon to select an ending date. All card requests that are older than the selected date will be purged from the history information:

Select Ending Date: [   ] 📅

[Purge Old Requests]

[Back to Maintenance Page]

Current Number of Saved Requests: 5

CARD REQUESTS

	REQUESTED ON	NAME	PHONE	STUDENT STATUS	CARD NUMBER
VIEW	12/12/2002	Frank D Post	(111) 111-1111	NO	123456789
VIEW	1/16/2003	Fred R Jones	(317) 222-1234	NO	123456789
VIEW	2/16/2003	Todd D Cutler	(317) 446-6979	NO	987654321
VIEW	2/16/2003	Rob S Cullin	(317) 509-3266	NO	987654321
VIEW	2/16/2003	Doug P Keaton	(317) 565-6555	NO	987654321

[Back to Maintenance Page]

Built in to the system is the ability to use multiple temporary library card numbers. Every week the system moves to the next available card number and uses it as the card number for that week. This can give the illusion that the temporary card numbers expire when in fact they do not. If a library should decide that this is not a factor, a single card number can be entered and the system will use it repeatedly.

The staff has the option to control the card numbers by using the Card Number Entry Maintenance Page. This page allows the staff to enter a new card number that is added to the list, edit existing card numbers, and delete existing numbers. This list is stored in a Card List table that contains two critical fields, "Card Number" and "ID." The "Card Number" field is used for storing the card numbers that the staff enters. The "ID" field contains a unique identification number associated with each card number. Another field was added to provide a time stamp for when the card number was added to the list, for record-keeping purposes. Figure 9.5 is an example of the Card Number Entry Maintenance Page.

The system uses the Card List table in conjunction with a Card Information table in order to issue the appropriate library card number. The Card Information table contains "Card Number," "Card ID," and "Expires" fields. The actual card number that is used for the week is

FIGURE 9.5   Card Number Entry Maintenance Page

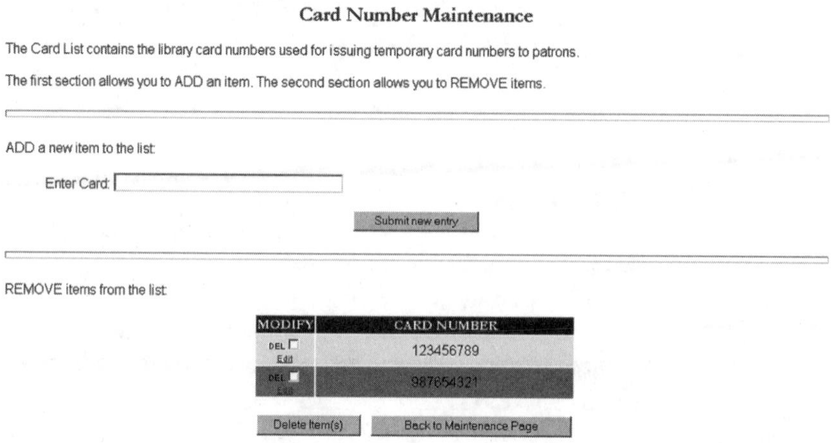

Card Number Maintenance

The Card List contains the library card numbers used for issuing temporary card numbers to patrons.

The first section allows you to ADD an item. The second section allows you to REMOVE items.

ADD a new item to the list:

Enter Card: [   ]

[Submit new entry]

REMOVE items from the list:

MODIFY	CARD NUMBER
DEL ☐ Edit	123456789
DEL ☑ Edit	987654321

[Delete Item(s)]   [Back to Maintenance Page]

stored in the "Card Number" field. The expiration date and time for the card number are stored in the "Expires" field. The system is programmed to use a new temporary card number every week. In this case, the system is programmed to use a new card starting every Saturday night at 12:00:01 a.m. There is no timer available to automatically have the system update the Card Information table with the next available card number. This is where the "Expires" field in the Card Information table is used. Once a request is submitted, the system does a quick check and compares the value in the "Expires" field in the Card Information table to the current date and time. If the current date is not past the expiration date, then the system issues the patron the card number that is stored in the Card Information table. If the current date is past the expiration date, then the card number needs to be updated. The system will use the "Card ID" value to find the next available ID value in the Card List table. The ID value provides the associated card number from the "Card Number" field. The new expiration date is calculated and the Card Information table is then updated with the new card number, ID number, and expiration date. The system then issues the patron the new temporary library card. The only requirement is that at least one card number must be stored in the Card List table. The ability to maintain a list of library card numbers and rotate them are optional elements of the system but provide flexibility.

The temporary library card issuing system is a convenient way for potential patrons who want to use the library's online services and do not have a library card to quickly receive a temporary library card number.

Those patrons who follow up to receive a permanent library card receive the convenience twice. Because they have already entered their information, the staff member only has to cut and paste the information for the temporary card system into the permanent card system. The patron does not have to wait while the staff member retypes all of her information into the system. In addition to offering convenience to potential patrons, the system offers the library a method to track those patrons who are using the online systems but do not have a library card. The library can use that information to reach out to those people to make sure they know about the other programs and services that the library has to offer.

10 Stand-Alone Services

*Bookmarklets, Proxy Servers,
and Electronic Reference*

Many of the products that we have discussed have involved systems, modules, or various scripting elements working together, but that doesn't always have to be the case. Innovative tools can be developed without the development of a large system.

BOOKMARKLETS

Jon Udell, the lead analyst at *InfoWorld*'s test center, has created a great new "bookmarklet" tool called LibraryLookup. Bookmarklets are free tools that extend the search capabilities of Explorer and Netscape web browsers. LibraryLookup is a JavaScript tool that allows an individual to see whether a book that is found on a bookseller's website is held in the local library collection. (Information on LibraryLookup is available at http://weblog.infoworld.com/udell/stories/2002/12/11/librarylookup.html.)

If you are one of those shoppers who finds books irresistible, and Amazon.com's huge inventory and services feed your frenzy, here is a way to put some brakes on. As you are browsing a bookseller's website, you can check to see whether the local library has a copy of the titles that you want, and possibly save a few bucks by borrowing them instead of buying them. This is a great no-cost marketing tool for local libraries as well. The way it works is that a LibraryLookup link is added to the individual's web browser toolbar. When the user finds a book of interest on a bookseller's web page, she simply clicks the LibraryLookup link. The JavaScript then scans that web page for the book item's ISBN (International Standard Book Number). If an ISBN is found, the bookmarklet sends the ISBN to the preferred library catalog and searches the catalog by ISBN. If the book is in the library database, the resulting item record is displayed in a new browser window. What makes this exciting is that a patron can find a book of interest on any bookseller's site, such as Amazon or Barnes & Noble, and with just a click of a mouse, she can find out whether her library has the same book.

The only catch is that the library's automation vendor must allow searching by ISBN. While not all library vendors support searching by ISBN, Innovative Interfaces, Endeavor's Voyager, Dynix's Horizon Information Portal (formerly epixtech's iPac), DRA, and Talis do support this feature. Udell's web page contains some bookmarklets already created for some of the libraries that use these vendors. Udell provides a formula for creating bookmarklets as well. A library can create and post the necessary bookmarklet link on its website. A patron can then drag and drop it onto his web browser's toolbar, and he is ready to search the library's catalog for an ISBN found on a web page. A *Library Journal* article raised this interesting question: "Udell's neat solution goes to the heart of a historic argument: do lending libraries detract from booksellers' profits, or do they help by creating readers and promoting titles?"[1] While others may debate the philosophical issues, the bookmarklet is a handy tool for patrons to use.

PROXY SERVERS

In contrast to the temporary library cards being used to access various online subscription services, a tighter degree of control is required by some online services. They don't want anybody and everybody to have access to their online services through the library's website. Only patrons of the library are allowed to gain access to the subscription database from home.

Many online subscription services allow access by recognizing the library's IP address or a range of IP addresses assigned to the library. This method works fine for computers within the library that access the services. Library computers can be configured to use the appropriate IP address or addresses, and this in turn allows direct access to the services. However, another step is required in order to provide the service to patrons at home. Patrons outside the library are using their own Internet connections, which have unique IP addresses assigned by an Internet service provider. Because these IP addresses are not within the range of the library's IP addresses, the patron will be denied access by the online subscription service.

A piece of software called a "proxy server" can be used to redirect authorized patrons to the online service by translating the patron's IP address to an appropriate library IP address. The online service sees the connection as if it was originating from the library and allows the patron access.

REMOTE-ACCESS SOFTWARE PACKAGES

EZproxy
http://www.usefulutilities.com/new/

Squid
http://www.squid-cache.org/

Apache
http://httpd.apache.org/docs/mod/mod_proxy.html

Netscape Proxy Server
http://wp.netscape.com/proxy/v3.5/

DeleGate
http://www.delegate.org/delegate/

See also "Remote User Authentication in Libraries"
http://library.smc.edu/rpa.htm

EZproxy is one of the software programs available that allows libraries to provide patrons with remote access to online subscription databases. It runs on both Linux and Windows and provides for a variety of ways to authenticate a user, one of which is to set the starting prefix and number of characters for the library card number. The software also allows for interaction with an external script, which can provide a platform for doing patron authentication against the library's automation database. In any case, once the library card number is accepted, the software connects to the online service using the library's valid IP address and routes the returned information back to the patron. This access to the online subscription service is allowed because the requests are originating from a valid library IP address. The process is seamless for the patron and provides the necessary authentication to make the connection. According to EZproxy's website, "EZproxy has been successfully used with databases provided by Britannica, EBSCO, FirstSearch, IAC (Gale), Lexis-Nexis, Newsbank, Ovid, SilverPlatter, SIRS, Softline and UMI, along with many others." This is a method that can be used for those online subscription services that allow the library to provide outside access to their services as part of the license agreement. (Some subscription service licenses require the patron to be physically at the library.)

EZproxy is only one example of a proxy server that can provide access to online subscription services. There is a web page titled "Remote User Authentication in Libraries" on the Santa Monica College Library website (http://library.smc.edu/rpa.htm). The page contains a variety of links pertaining to proxy servers and authentication, ranging from general information to specific information pertaining to libraries and colleges.

ELECTRONIC REFERENCE SERVICE

Reference service is making a shift to electronic media along with library customer behavior. "Electronic reference service" is an umbrella term for many different forms of reference service. These include e-mail reference, digital reference, online reference, virtual reference, asynchronous online reference, and collaborative reference, among others. The common thread in all these processes is that technology—specifically, the Web—is used to provide reference service to a remote user. They are all interactive services. In some cases, the customer receives the service in "real time," right when he or she needs the information. In other cases, time elapses and the interaction is one more step removed from the customer, as with e-mail reference. Electronic reference is a logical step for libraries to take in providing service to remote users. The traditional reference service model has included telephone reference to accomplish remote service for years.

E-Mail Reference

E-mail reference service is simple to establish and easy for patrons to understand. The e-mail address for the service is simply posted on the library website, and a staff member is designated to monitor the requests. E-mail queries from customers are routed to the specified staff person, who is responsible for either answering the reference question or routing it to other staff. The disadvantage of e-mail reference is that several e-mails between the librarian and the patron may be required to be sure that the librarian understands the question. E-mail reference transactions are typically tracked by the number of questions received, and the time required for answering them. Both e-mail reference and web form reference are also referred to as "asynchronous online reference."

Web Form-Based Reference Service

This form of electronic reference is another type of e-mail reference. Forms are available on the library website for the submission of questions. The forms typically ask for the customer's e-mail address and may or may not be structured to narrow the questioner's focus somewhat, in order to reduce initial ambiguities of the reference transaction. These transactions are typically tracked in the same way that e-mail transactions are tracked.

ONLINE REFERENCE PRODUCTS

Reference software packages vary widely in price. Contact vendors for online demos and in-house trials to be sure that the software is compatible with your existing library software.

24/7 Reference
www.247ref.org

Convey's OnDemand
www.conveysystems.com

LSSI's Virtual Reference Software
www.lssi.com

LiveAssistance
www.liveassistance.com

LiveHelper
www.livehelper.com

LivePerson, Inc.
www.liveperson.com

NetMeeting
www.microsoft.com/windows/
    netmeeting/home

Live Online Reference Services

Live online reference services provide real-time reference help over the Internet. These services include such methods as co-browsing, real-time reference, two-way chat, web push, and voice-over IP, among others. These services have emerged in libraries as a result of their success in commercial business models. Similar software, called "customer relationship management" software, or CRM, has been used in the private sector to learn about customer needs and purchasing patterns in order to provide better service.

The first of these methods is co-browsing. "Collaborative browsing (also known as co-browsing) is a software-enabled technique that allows someone in an enterprise contact center to interact with a customer by using the customer's web browser to show them something"; it effectively allows the librarian and the customer to be "on the same page."[2] The librarian can take control of the customer's web browser for demonstration purposes.

Web push technology, also called "page push technology," is a form of content sharing between the librarian and the customer. It provides a way for the librarian to push a live website to the remote customer's web browser, as opposed to a static screen shot. The librarian can type a URL in on his screen and with a button click, the page will either appear on the remote customer's screen or it will appear in a new browser window, depending on the software used.

In two-way chat, also known as "instant messaging," the librarian communicates with the customer through a text window on the screen. Two-way chat can sometimes be awkward and clumsy as a method of handling a reference transaction, but it is the most prevalent form of online reference currently used.

Voice-over IP (voice-over Internet Protocol) provides two-way voice communication between the customer and the librarian. It requires speakers and microphones at both ends of the transaction, a high-speed connection, and software that supports the application, in addition to configuration at the patron's end. Audio and video technologies have improvements to make before they will replace online chat, but most experts agree that they will eventually replace text-based reference systems.

For a complete discussion of online reference, see the following publications:

Nancy K. Maxwell, "Establishing and Maintaining Live Online Reference Service," *Library Technology Reports* 38, no. 4 (July/August 2002).

Steve Coffman, *Going Live: Starting and Running a Virtual Reference Service* (Chicago: American Library Association, 2003).

Live online reference service is by far the most highly discussed and hyped form of reference service today. There are high expectations for live online reference within the library profession, and some librarians are very enthusiastic about participating in it. Others, however, are considering getting involved only because they feel it is a necessity in order to avoid being left behind. In some cases, librarians are turning to digital reference in reaction to a dip in traditional library reference use, as patrons head to the Internet with all of its promise. Many of these patrons, when they get to the Web, find they need help in navigating it, and this is where live online reference shines. Consider the bemused patron who is trying to decode the expert search form for an online database: "hmmmm. Boolean what?!" He has already typed in his search term and received disappointing (or overwhelming) results. He doesn't need an "Expert Search" at this point; he needs an expert! And by this we mean a live expert. It makes sense that if our customers are going to be on the Web, we need to be there as well. If we are not available, someone else will be. There are many commercial companies and nonprofit organizations offering online reference software and support services that have no affiliation with libraries. Libraries are uniquely qualified to offer better service in this arena because we have highly trained and professional personnel to provide the assistance.

IMPLEMENTING LIVE ONLINE REFERENCE SERVICE

Libraries thinking about testing the live online reference waters will need to decide whether they want local control of the service. The other option is to join a collaborative service group. The software can be licensed for local control or it can be outsourced to either a vendor's call center or a library digital reference consortium. Many things factor into this decision, including staff size, expertise, and availability; hours of operation; and the size of the community to which the service will be provided, to name just a few.

Cooperative Services

Cooperative live online reference services resolve some of the scheduling problems of providing 24-hour reference service, 7 days a week. Libraries that participate in a cooperative service have a scheduling flexibility that is not possible for independently managed services. They can take advantage of time zones, for instance, so that the early morning time slot is staffed by a librarian in another time zone. The disadvantage of a cooperative service is that some libraries have misgivings about having local questions answered remotely.

Independent Services

Libraries may choose to manage all aspects of a live online reference service independently. The largest issue with this is that the library's own reference staff must be available to provide the service, and this can be a problem for an online reference service that is staffed on a 24/7 basis. Libraries considering this option will need to decide whether to use the existing reference desk staff or create a separate staff for online service provision. This determination may involve some trial and error and adjustments, and many human resource issues are involved.

In either case, libraries must decide how they will control who gets to use the digital reference service. Users must be authenticated in some way, whether by library card, PIN, digital certificate, or some other means.

Notes

1. "LibraryLookup: Go to Amazon, Find Library Book," *Library Journal* (21 January 2003), available at http://libraryjournal.reviewsnews.com/index.asp?layout=article&articleid=CA271236&display=InfoTechNews&industry=InfoTech&industryid=1988&verticalid=151&publication=libraryjournal (accessed 1 February 2003).
2. Definition of "collaborative browsing" by searchCRM.com.

11 Marketing Web-Based Library Services

REACHING OUT TO NON-USERS AND USERS ALIKE

Okay! So you have a terrific new technology-based service. You have a patron service base of, well, thousands . . . and a patron database of thousands too. You need to let them *all* know about the new technology service, and more importantly, you need to get them to use it. With the exception of the overdue notice strategy covered later in this chapter, all of the marketing tactics suggested here can be used to reach both library users and non-users. The goal is saturation. If you've ever sat on the sidelines at a library focus group for the library that employs you, you're likely to have come away somewhat frustrated. Typically, despite the library's very best efforts at marketing, there are still an alarming number of people in the community who have no idea what programs, services, and materials the library has to offer. Members of the focus group will say that they wish the library was open on Sundays (when it already is), or they wish it held programs for three- to five-year-olds (when it has been doing so for years), or they wish it had books on tape available for checkout (when it does). It's difficult to get people's attention nowadays. It would be nice to know a foolproof formula for getting the attention of your community, but in lieu of that, here are some suggestions that have worked for various libraries. These suggestions are for marketing technology-based library services, but most will work for other services and projects as well.

Marketing Services to Library Users

Newsletters

There are a few obvious, tried and true venues for getting the word about anything new out to the community. The first of these is the library newsletter. Many libraries print a monthly newsletter, and this is a great vehicle for marketing a library's new technology service. A front-page article in the newsletter is likely to be seen by most of the people who take the time to look at the newsletter.

These folks comprise a specific patron group; they are probably already committed library users and pretty good library supporters. If they are picking the newsletter up in the library to read it at home, they very likely will get the information about the new technology service highlighted in the newsletter issue. They are already library users. But the group to which you mail the newsletter bears a little closer scrutiny. Who are they, really? Why do you mail the newsletter to them? How many of them do you mail it to? Of that group, how many are "professional courtesy" mailings, such as other library directors, administrators, and so on? How many are bona fide patrons who have requested to be added to the newsletter mailing list? Is the mailing list a compilation of other mailing lists, like the one for the chamber of commerce members or the community foundation's mailing list? Ask yourself how you assembled the list, in order to get a clearer snapshot of the community you are actually reaching. Many libraries run reports on their automation system to assemble such lists. For example, they may have a list of the top 500 book circulators for the past year. These patrons may receive a newsletter regardless of whether they have requested it, on the assumption that they would be interested. This is a perfectly legitimate method for generating mailing databases, but when it is a specific service that you are targeting, it is also sometimes a specific population that you are targeting, and some scrutiny of the newsletter mailing list may be in order. Databases can be easily created in-house to target specific groups, such as the top 500 book circulators for the year, or a database of the names of everyone who has registered for a technology class in the past year. These can comprise a mailing list, and postcards advertising the new technology service can easily be sent to each name in the database at little cost, simply by generating address labels from the mailing list.

Another method to get a little more mileage from the newsletter is to publish a front-page article in it the first month, followed by monthly articles targeted at specific user groups within the community. For example, if the newsletter features a regular Adult Services page, an article on that page could highlight the ways that the new technology service specifically benefits adult library patrons. The following month, an article on the Young Adult Services page could invite those young adult users to try the service. This article could tie in to other technology services that young adult patrons may be interested in. It's important to make the new technology service personally relevant to the particular groups the library has designated as target groups in order to get those individuals interested enough to try it.

Interactive Websites as a Marketing Tool

Interactive websites like that of the Public Library of Charlotte and Mecklenburg County (http://www.plcmc.org/default.htm) are marketing tools in and of themselves. As patrons both young and old become familiar with the options and services available from the website, the library's value to them is increased. To cite a few examples, the "Classic Fairy Tale Ebooks" link on the website of the Auckland (New Zealand) City Libraries (http://www.aucklandlibrary.co.nz/process.asp?pageurl=index.html) is a site that young kids would want to return to again and again. The site does a great job of combining the idea of libraries with having fun and being able to do a lot of neat things. "Kids' Corner" on the Calgary Public Library site (http://calgarypubliclibrary.com/kids/music.htm) offers games and animated picture books with audio. The Baltimore County Public Library website (http://www.bcplonline.org/index.html) provides e-mail accounts and hosting for personal web pages.

A new technology service is likely to reside on your website and probably has a button. However, scrolling banners or flashing buttons can help to bring attention to the new service during its introductory stage. It helps to jazz things up a bit until you know you have gotten people's attention.

E-Mail Advertising

Many automation vendors include an option for e-mail overdue notification as part of their systems. In most cases, the text of the e-mail notice is easy to change. It could easily include notice of the new technology service, and would reach an audience who already uses technology and might welcome the chance to try the new service. The e-mail may be able to link to the new technology service if it is available from the website, or it may be able to link to a page on the library website that provides more information about the service. The library website is also a good place to advertise the new technology service. A scrolling banner can easily be created to link to an information page that introduces and explains the service.

In-House Promotion

Within the library, staff can wear buttons advertising the new service, and bookmarks can be distributed to each patron. Never underestimate the power of word of mouth! Enthusiastic circulation staff members are in an ideal position to inform each patron of the availability of a new service. This can be a huge boost to your marketing efforts. Even a single really enthusiastic staffer can spread the word of the new web service to a large number of patrons on a busy day. Train your circulation staff in the use of the new technology service so they are comfortable talking about it. Give them a script, since, in addition to being pleasant and welcoming, they have many other things to remember in any given circulation transaction.

A simple script, in the form of a bookmark that highlights components of the service with bullet-points, will make it a lot easier for them to give accurate information to each patron. Think about having circulation staff distribute color copies of small screen prints that indicate where a web-based service resides on the library's website. It's important to remember that users need to be able to find the new service if it is web-enabled. Screen prints can make the task of initially finding the service on the website that much simpler for patrons.

One way to save money on bookmark production is to print them in-house, but libraries can also consider having a printer produce multiple "shells" of bookmarks for subsequent additional printing in-house. Shells consist of regular 8½ × 11-inch sheets on which multiple bookmarks are printed. These bookmarks can be standardized with the library logo or the library website address and a colorful graphic, or with the library's hours of operation. White space is left for subsequent printing in-house to address special promotions or details of new services. The advantage to the library is that a printer can print a thousand or several thousand shells at a relatively low price, and the library still gets to vary the copy on the bookmarks by adding copy selectively, in-house, as needed. It is worthwhile to consider hiring an advertising agency to come up with a great layout for the shells, which can be used over and over again, for as long as the library would like. The cost of the design work is usually reasonable when leveraged over the number of pieces that will make their way into the hands of community members.

Balloons and banners are upbeat attention-getters for advertising new services to in-house patrons. These same tools can be used outside the library as well. Consider duplicating the color scheme of the library website or the logo of the new service on a large number of balloons or a couple of banners, and display these props each time the library establishes a presence at school or community events. And seriously consider advertising the new technology service at community events. Get a booth, or have a local merchant sponsor a booth for the library, where the main story can be the new technology service.

Marketing Services to Non-Users

Community Partnerships: Businesses

Including local merchants as a marketing venue for a new technology service is a winning situation for both the merchants and the library. Most local businesses recognize that the library is good for the community, and most businesses are glad to be associated with the "forward-thinking" ideas that technology engenders. Like it or not, our patrons are also consumers. Many librarians oppose the idea of referring to patrons as "customers," but increasingly they are behaving like customers. As the range of service and product options offered by libraries increases, so do the expectations of our patrons. It's time to start thinking more like retailers. Business models were discussed in chapter 2, and libraries have clearly learned some important lessons from such retailers as Amazon.com. But libraries also need to start thinking about how retailers utilize their local spaces to advertise special discounts or new items to shoppers. Libraries can learn some valuable marketing techniques from retailers that are useful when developing a plan to market new technology-based services.

Retailers use every available space to reach their customers. Banners and signs are hung from the ceiling; posters are strategically placed on both display fixtures and product fixtures. And if you are a particularly alert consumer, you may have noticed that grocery merchants are now leasing their actual floor space to vendors; there are floor decals that advertise particular brands on the floor of many large grocery stores. These change on a rotating basis, depending on which product distributor has the contract for promotion. Years back, during the heyday of the juvenile *Goosebumps* horror series, Scholastic Publishing's retail promotional packet for the series included a set of several huge, orange, monster-shaped feet with sticky-backs that a retailer could affix to the floor to lead customers to the *Goosebumps* books. It's this kind of surprising marketing tactic that gets the attention of consumers, and it's this kind of marketing plan that libraries compete with in the attention marketplace.

Retailers also tend to use any window space available to them, especially since walls are often taken up by product storage and display. Window slicks are an option to offer to local retail partners, where merchants may not have much retail floor space to offer. This kind of partnership works well for small to medium-size library communities, where the central library is easily accessible from most locations in town. On a busy street that sees a lot of sidewalk traffic, attractive window slicks can be especially effective, as long as their message is kept simple and bright. Increasing numbers of retailers see library partnerships as good business, so the opportunity is there for libraries to get a lot more exposure.

Partnering with local retailers will leverage your resources and make the most of your advertising budget. It will help you to reach people who would otherwise be difficult to reach, since they may not be using the library. In addition to extending your reach, partnering with local merchants improves community relationships and elevates the library's profile in the community. If your community or visitor's bureau has a website, or if you are a member of the local chamber of commerce, a link to the new service from their pages is an easy technique to introduce the service to new users, the business community, and new members of the community.

Whether your library is contacting all or only a portion of its delinquent patrons with standard snail-mail overdue notices, the text of the overdue notice is worth considering as an advertising opportunity as well. A brief announcement of the new technology service can be programmed to appear at the end of the overdue notice. Or an advertising flyer announcing the new service can be included in the envelope with the overdue notice for as little as the cost of flyer duplication. Stickers advertising the service can be placed on the envelopes, or the website address and service logo can be printed or stamped on the envelopes.

Community Partnerships: Schools

Here's a captive audience! School newsletters can provide for a great partnership opportunity between schools and libraries. Often the overlap in coverage between students and library patrons is just what's needed to ensure that information actually gets out to students and their families. If you have the opportunity to distribute the school corporation newsletter at the library, it can be a great trade-off by which to get a little library publicity in the school newsletter. If students are part of the target population for your library's new technology service, consider doing a spot or a full-length interview on the student-directed, closed-circuit television program that many high schools produce. If the local park district produces a monthly or annual guide, it can be another great advertising opportunity for the library, as well as another opportunity to "trade" advertising.

Within the school–library partnership realm, don't forget about teachers. Within the classroom audience segment, teachers are king, and their influence is important. If you can get local teachers to urge students to try the new technology service, or better yet, give students extra credit for their use of the service, it will go a long way to clearing the highest hurdle in technology adoption: that of getting customers to try the new technology.

Newspaper Advertising

Newspaper advertising is often a default marketing venue. The obvious advantage of newspaper ads is that they are available to a large readership. The disadvantage is that newspaper advertising can be expensive to maintain for any length of time, and it is difficult to control the placement of the ad. The customer often does not have the opportunity to choose whether his ad shows up on the obituary page, the back page of the city/state section, or the sports section. Given these circumstances, there is really no substitute for a great relationship with local newspapers, which can pave the way to a little leverage on ad placement. Be sure to ask the classified advertising department *where* the ad will be placed, and get it in writing if possible. Libraries should also consider using a display advertising format. A display ad is a type of classified advertisement that involves clip art or graphics. If you have a lot to say or the text in your ad is lengthy, a display ad is a way to make it look cleaner and more attractive. Sometimes newspapers will offer special discounts on display ads in order to get more advertisers to try them. Even if a special discount is not available, they are a more effective way to advertise and are worth considering.

If you choose to use newspaper ads as a method to advertise the new technology service, think about looking for local funding for the ads. Local businesses that cannot offer retail floor or window space may be willing to underwrite newspaper advertising for nothing more than the addition of their tagline at the bottom of the ad. A manufacturing company that does not have enough in-house, retail-type traffic to function as an effective advertising venue is still a good candidate for the funding of newspaper advertising.

Another local business that may consider underwriting the cost of the ads is the newspaper itself. If you plan the technology promotion to run for a predetermined length of time, consider approaching your local paper for advertising dollars. This sort of "in kind" funding is easy for the paper to write off, and it will be more likely to agree to come on board if it knows there is a definite beginning and end to the promotion. As you meet with the Friends of the Library, let them know how important it is to support your new technology services with solid advertising. Ask the Friends group to budget for advertising of the new service.

Billboard Advertising

And finally, be willing to experiment! The Mooresville Library leased a billboard beside a busy interstate highway passing through the center of the library district in order to advertise its new automatic e-mail service. Louisiana's LOUIS system, a statewide library consortium of 120 public, school, and academic libraries, advertised its home page with a billboard campaign funded by the Gale Group. LOUIS offered an extensive list of online databases and resources on its website for statewide access. Billboard advertising text should be kept simple and to a minimum. Billboard companies have a design department that will assist you in the development of your billboard design. They will collect your ideas and requirements and will submit several designs from which the library can choose. While the impact of billboard advertising is difficult to quantify, it is clearly a simple and powerful way to get a message out to commuters.

What to Say

When choosing advertising text for your technology-based service, take care to choose text that is appropriate for each particular target group. For instance, if you want to market your library gateway to school-age children, think about how they will be using it and promote those particular aspects of the product. If you want to market the gateway to seniors and local history buffs, promote those specific resource options in your advertising copy. This may seem like a no-brainer, but many times a single advertising line is chosen and that same ad copy is used for all promotional materials. Remember that these days, one size rarely fits all. In the drive to customization and personalization, people really want to know "What does it do for *me; why should *I* use it?" There has to be a good reason for users to adopt the technology, and to ride the learning curve until they are able to use it with ease. Some library customers will need to be convinced of the benefits and merits of technology-based services before they try them.

MEASURING RESULTS

Marketing campaigns get the word out, but how do we know if they work or not? In the case of a web-based service, this can be accomplished by measuring the website's traffic. Traditionally, hit counters have provided a means of measurement. With a glance, the library staff can see how many hits have been made to the home page. But the counter can be misleading, and it does not tell you who has been hitting the website. Many libraries set the default home page of the web browsers on their in-house computers to point to the library's website. Often the staff members also set the default home page on their computers to the library website. Every time a web browser is started, another hit is registered to the website. Multiplying the number of in-house computers times the number of instances a single browser on an in-house computer is started throughout a day will yield the number of internal hits that are registered to the website. This is not really a good means of measurement, since the library has no way of knowing whether the hit count represents internal staff use, internal patron use, or external patron use.

Web servers like IIS and Apache have become more sophisticated over the years. They provide a means of logging data about hits to the website, such as those hits' date, time, the IP address of the client, and the object requested. The web server can be configured with regard to how often a new data log file is made available, such as hourly, daily, monthly, and so on. The raw files are generally difficult to parse through because they are a long list of every request that was made to or from pages on the website while the log file was active. This can amount to hundreds or even thousands of requests over a day's time.

Luckily, there is software available that does the parsing and analysis of the log files and provides the data in consolidated, readable formats. Software programs like wwwstat (http://ftp.ics.uci.edu/pub/websoft/wwwstat/) and NetTracker (http://www.sane.com/products/NetTracker/) look through the data stored in the log file and provide useful information. A variety of freeware and purchased or subscription software is available that does this. The primary purpose of such products is to consolidate information in the log file and provide useful statistics. These statistics include the number of requests by client domain; that is, how many .net, .com, .us, and so on have requested items on the website. Other key pieces of information that these products provide are a list of the domain addresses that hit the website, how many requests for information were made by those domain addresses, and how many requests were made for each page. The breakdown of where the requests originate helps to weed out those that are generated from within the library, so that a true analysis can be done of where the outside requests are coming from. The IP addresses and URLs that are captured do not necessarily point you back to specific patrons, but they can be checked on the Web to see who they belong to.

Some addresses are more obvious than others. If the IP address or URL belongs to a local Internet service provider, you can be more certain that a local patron was using the services. If the IP address or URL belongs to an out-of-state service provider or a googlebot, it may not be a local patron, but rather a search engine looking for information. Other IP and URL addresses can be more difficult to trace. In any case, tracking the number of requests by certain groups like .com, .net, .gov, and .us can provide trending information that corresponds to specific ad and marketing campaigns. This trending information can be examined to determine whether the overall website traffic increases in correlation to the specific campaign. The specific web page request information can provide such statistics as the top ten lists of most visited web pages on the website. You can look at a specific web page and see how many requests were made. This is very useful information if, for example, a link to a new service resides on a specific web page. An increase in the number of hits to the web page will be an indication that people are finding the new service. Conversely, by analyzing the requests from a web page, you might find that a page containing a link to online services is not being utilized. This can indicate the need to generate a marketing campaign to raise awareness of the services and bring people to that page. In all cases, tracking website usage is a good way to gauge marketing and advertising effectiveness.

TECHNOLOGY READINESS CONSIDERATIONS

Many technology products fail not because of the technology but because the developers were not savvy about marketing them. It is important for libraries to understand the readiness profiles of their communities and the need to modify marketing to address successive waves of adopters. Each community is made up of groups of people with similar general levels of readiness to adopt new technology. A. Parasuraman and Charles Colby have categorized five groups of technology consumers that range from laggards through pioneers.[1] They theorize that the five groups of consumers have certain traits and attitudes and adopt new technology at different rates. The experience of many librarians bears this out even as we deal with patrons on the service floor. Each of us has known some patron who hates computers, distrusts technology, rues the day that the library ditched the card catalog, and refuses to use the OPAC. This technology curmudgeon still has lots of company, and as librarians we try to bring them along by providing the most basic of technology training sessions and by making sure that our public service staffs have the background to assist them.

Among our customers there is also likely to be a middle-of-the-road group comprised of people who are somewhat skeptical about new technology. This group might consider trying a new library technology service if they were convinced that it might have some personal relevance to them. But they are not usually very optimistic about technology services in general.

At the far end of the spectrum, we all have other patrons who love to explore new technology solutions. They are curious and interested in technology for its own sake, and they might try a new technology service regardless of whether it appeared to have any personal relevance to them. This group is very willing to try something new. They are very likely to be regular users of technology products and services and they may well be among our most highly wired customers.

These shared patron characteristics describe the attitudes with which various segments of our communities approach technology. Libraries have also seen that these segments will adopt new technology at different rates, ranging from rapid adoption to adoption at a snail's pace. These are valuable things to be reminded of as we launch a new technology service. If the service is ultimately successful, it is likely to be adopted over time, by successive "waves" of customers. Parasuraman and Colby found this to be the case over the lifetime of a unique technology in the business sector. The patron group that is the first to adopt a new technology service will probably comprise those customers who are the most enthusiastic about technology and are confident that they can make it work. But the more skeptical "middle-of-the-road" folks are not likely to try the new technology service until well into the game, and even then, only after they have been convinced that it offers some personal relevance to them. This is another reason to keep staff in the loop for such services as the online program registration. While many patrons will love being able to control their program registration, there will always be those who prefer to have someone else handle the task, or who have no intention of adopting the processes necessary to master the technology.

The lesson here is that any conclusions regarding the success of new technology services cannot be drawn overnight. Patrons who have a positive approach to new technology will be quick to adopt the new service, but an early assessment of the service's acceptance based only on this group's response may be premature. Less optimistic users will be slower to adopt the new service and will require more support and incentives to get them to try the service. This patron group will require a greater degree of coaxing, more personal relevancy from the service, and more hand-holding.

Libraries will need to consider reaching out to all of their customers when developing marketing for new technology services. The fact that there are different levels of technology readiness in our communities makes a case for a much more sustained marketing campaign, with varying approaches to reach the varying levels of optimism regarding the new product. The challenge is to be able to identify the technology readiness levels present in our individual library communities, and devise methods for marketing to each of them. At a minimum, libraries should recognize that varying levels of technology readiness do exist in their communities. Libraries like the Lakewood Public Library in Ohio have used demographic tools and market segmentation to learn more about their communities for marketing purposes, while the Richmond Public Library in British Columbia simply acted on customer requests on written comment cards.[2] Libraries can hire a marketing firm or hand-code and tabulate their own survey data. Either method of gathering community data will give you a snapshot of your community.

Notes

1. A. Parasuraman and Charles Colby, *Techno-Ready Marketing: How and Why Your Customers Adopt Technology* (New York: Free Press, 2001).
2. Evan St. Lifer and Andrew Albanese, "Tapping into the Zen of Marketing," *Library Journal* 126, no. 8 (1 May 2001): 47.

Bibliography

Arar, Yardena. "Starbucks Expands Wireless Internet Offering." *PC World* (21 August 2002).

Bannen, Karen J. "Personalization and Portals: If You Build It (Right) They Will Come." *EContent* 25, no. 10 (October 2002).

Boss, Richard W. "How to Plan and Implement a Library Portal," *Library Technology Reports* 38, no. 6 (November/December 2002).

Chia, Christopher, and June Garcia. "The Personalization Challenge in Public Libraries: Perspectives and Prospects." 2002. Available at http://www.bertelsmann-stiftung.de/documents/Personalisation_engl.pdf. Accessed 4 February 2003.

Cushing, K. "Instant Benefits (Instant Messaging)." *Computer Weekly* (18 July 2002): 24.

Dorman, David. "Open Source Software and the Intellectual Commons." *American Libraries* 33, no. 11 (December 2002): 51–54.

Forester, Leslie Ann. "Push Technology." *Legal Assistant Today* (May/June 1998): 36–37.

Hoffert, Barbara. "Book Report 2000: Circulation Dips but Buying Still Up." *Library Journal* 125, no. 3 (15 February 2000): 130–32.

———. "Book Report 2002: The Amazon Effect." *Library Journal* 127, no. 3 (15 February 2002): 38–40.

Hollowell, Todd. "Customers Want the Personal Touch." *Information Week* (24 June 2002): 48.

Jackson, Mary E. "The Advent of Portals." *Library Journal* 127, no. 15 (15 September 2002): 36–39.

Jones *e*-global library. "The Role of Librarians in the Digital Age." 2001. Available at http://www.jonesknowledge.com/eglobal/pdf/ala_survey_results.pdf. Accessed 14 November 2002.

Ketchell, Debra. "Too Many Channels: Making Sense Out of Portals and Personalization." *Information Technology and Libraries* 19, no. 4 (2000).

Kochtanek, Tom. "New Developments in Integrated Library Systems." *Library Technology* (November 2001). Available at http://gessler. emeraldinsight.com/vl=9528114/cl=114/nw=1/rpsv/librarylink/technology/nov01.htm#article. Accessed 29 November 2002.

"Library Lookup: Go to Amazon, Find Library Book." *Library Journal* (21 January 2003). Available at http://libraryjournal.reviewsnews. com/index.asp?layout=article&articleid=CA271236&display= InfoTechNews&industry=InfoTech&industryid=1988&verticalid= 151&publication=libraryjournal. Accessed 1 February 2003.

Looney, Michael, and Peter Lyman. "Portals in Higher Education." *EDUCAUSE Review* 35, no. 4 (July/August 2000). Available at http://www.educause.edu/ir/library/pdf/ERM0042.pdf. Accessed 10 February 2003.

Minkel, Walter. "Study: Summer Reading Helps Students." *School Library Journal* 48, no. 2 (February 2002): 24.

Morgan, Eric Lease. "The Challenges of User-Centered, Customizable Interfaces to Library Resources." *Information Technology and Libraries* 19, no. 4 (December 2000).

Morgan, Eric Lease, and Amy Ising. "My Library: A Manual and Workshop." 2000. Available at http://dewey.library.nd.edu/ mylibrary/manual/mylibrary-manual.html#id230857. Accessed 3 January 2003.

Nielsen, Jakob. "Personalization Is Over-Rated." 1998. Available at http:/www.useit.com/alertbox/981004.html. Accessed 10 February 2003.

Parasuraman, A., and Charles Colby. *Techno-Ready Marketing: How and Why Your Customers Adopt Technology.* New York: Free Press, 2001.

Pew Internet & American Life Project. "Counting on the Internet." 2002. Available at http://www.pewinternet.org/reports/toc. asp?Report=80. Accessed 9 January 2003.

———. "Getting Serious Online." 2002. Available at http://www. pewinternet.org/reports/toc.asp?Report=55. Accessed 12 December 2002.

———. "The Internet and Education." 2001. Available at http://www.pewinternet.org/reports/toc.asp?Report=39. Accessed 9 January 2003.

Saveniji, Bas, and Natalia Grygierczyk. "Libraries without Resources: Towards Personal Collections." *Collection Building* 20, no. 1 (2001): 18–24.

"The Shifted Librarian" [home page of Jenny Levine]. Available at http://www.theshiftedlibrarian.com/stories/2002/01/19/whatIs AShiftedLibrarian.html. Accessed 3 January 2003.

St. Lifer, Evan, and Andrew Albanese. "Tapping into the Zen of Marketing." *Library Journal* 126, no. 8 (1 May 2001): 44–47.

"Technology and Library Users: LITA Experts Identify Trends to Watch." 1999. Available at http://www.lita.org/committe/toptech/ trendsmw99.htm. Accessed 12 December 2002.

Tennant, Roy. "Digital Libraries—The Convenience Catastrophe." *Library Journal* 126, no. 20 (15 December 2001): 39–40.

Thomas, Sarah E. "The Catalog as Portal to the Internet." 21 December 2000. Available at http://lcweb.loc.gov/catdir/bibcontrol/ thomas_paper.html. Accessed 11 January 2003.

"Thus Said." *American Libraries* (December 2002): 41.

Wilson, Ray, and Paul Harsin. *Process Mastering: How to Establish and Document the Best Known Way to Do a Job.* New York: Quality Resources, 1998.

Zeithaml, Valarie. *Delivering Quality Service.* New York: Simon and Schuster, 1990.

Index

LYNN JUREWICZ is the director of the Mooresville Public Library in a suburb of Indianapolis, Indiana. She has professional experience in both academic and public libraries. Jurewicz's background in both technical and public services has provided her with an understanding of the limitations of widely available automated systems, as well as a sense of their possibilities. She has authored articles about technology, school–public library cooperation, and director–board relationships for the *Indiana Libraries* journal, and has presented those topics at PLA and ALA conferences. She received her M.L.S. degree from Kent State University.

TODD CUTLER is the president and founder of E*vanced Solutions. He spent fourteen years as a product engineer designing software and electronic devices for automating industrial applications. Since 2000, his focus has shifted to providing automated solutions for various areas within public libraries, using the skills he developed in the industrial automation market. He has given presentations at various conferences on the topic of automating manual tasks within the library, and he continues to provide innovative solutions and custom applications for the various manual tasks that libraries perform day to day.